NUTRIBULLET RECIPE BOOK

500+ Inspiring and Health-Boosting Recipes for Balanced and Energized Life with Every Mood and Occasion

By

Derrick C. Virgen

TABLE OF CONTENT

CHAPTER 5: PROTEIN-POWERED SMOOTHIE CREATIONS 43

CHAPTER 6: DAIRY-FREE AND VEGAN SMOOTHIE DELIGHTS 58

CHAPTER 17: SEASONAL SMOOTHIE SPECIALTIES 189

CHAPTER 18: QUICK AND EASY ON-THE-GO SMOOTHIES...............................200

This book explores the amazing world of mixing delectable and nutritious concoctions and digs into indigsthe art of Nutribullet smoothies. Due to its adaptability, practicality, and health advantages, smoothies have recently experienced tremendous growth in popularity. You can up your smoothie game with the Nutribullet, a potent and effective blender. The benefits and opportunities offered by the Nutribullet smoothie experience are highlighted in this chapter, which serves as an introduction.

The Popularity of Smoothies: First, we'll talk about how quickly and healthfully smoothies have become popular meal choices. Smoothies have become a mainstay in many people's diets, including busy professionals, families, fitness fanatics, and health-conscious people. We examine the factors contributing to this trend, including smoothies' practicality, diversity, and adaptability.

The Nutribullet is now available: The Nutribullet is a premium blender known for its strong engine, effective extraction system, and user-friendly design. We examine the Nutribullet's attributes and parts, including the motor base, extractor blade, cups, and lids. Amazing smoothies can be made after you understand how the Nutribullet functions.

Benefits of Nutribullet Smoothies: In this part, we examine the many advantages of creating smoothies in a Nutribullet. We discuss the Nutribullet's potent motor and extraction abilities, guaranteeing a smoother blend and improved texture and consistency. Additionally, the high-speed blending function of the Nutribullet preserves more nutrients and enzymes from the ingredients, boosting the health advantages of each smoothie.

The Science of Smoothies: Made in a NutriBullet Understanding the science underlying the blending procedure is essential to appreciate the art of Nutribullet smoothies fully. The design of the Nutribullet improves the release and absorption of nutrients from fruits, vegetables, and other components as we examine the principles of extraction and nutrient retention. This section aims to help the reader comprehend the nutritional benefits of Nutribullet smoothies.

Essential Blender Smoothie Ingredients: Let's examine the main components that give Nutribullet smoothies great flavor and nutrient-dense concentration. We look at various fruits, veggies, leafy greens, nuts, seeds, and other additions that can improve your smoothies' nutritional profile and flavor. We offer a thorough list of ingredients to help you create the perfect smoothie, from protein-rich Greek yogurt to antioxidant-rich berries.

Balancing Flavor and Nutrition: When making a smoothie, it's essential to consider flavor and nutrition. This section discusses the value of adding items that provide a variety of essential vitamins, minerals, and macronutrients, as well as balancing sweet and savory flavors. We offer pointers and techniques for creating the ideal flavor profile while ensuring your smoothies are nutrient-diverse.

Tips for Successful Nutribullet Smoothies: We provide a variety of helpful pointers and advice to help you get the most out of your blender and produce delicious smoothies. We give tips to improve your blending experience, from carefully stacking ingredients to reaching the right consistency. We also offer advice on serving quantities, appropriate liquid proportions, and ways to make smoothies with various textures.

The Art of Presentation: In our final section, we'll talk about how to showcase your NutriBullet smoothies. Although taste and nutrition should come first, a smoothie's aesthetic appeal can improve the experience. We discuss garnishing, stacking, and decorating smoothies to enhance their aesthetic appeal. We inspire you to improve your smoothie appearance, from vibrant fruit slices and fresh herbs to original glassware and toppings for smoothie bowls.

Troubleshooting and Typical Obstacles: Making a smoothie can occasionally be difficult, so we want to ensure you're ready. This section tackles frequent problems during the blending process, such as obtaining the proper consistency, avoiding separation, or handling excessively thick or thin smoothies. We offer troubleshooting advice and methods to solve these issues and guarantee smoothie success each time.

Making Smoothies a Part of Your Lifestyle: The chapter's conclusion discusses including smoothies made with a Nutribullet into your everyday activities and way of life. We advise including smoothies in your meal planning, balancing smoothie intake with substantial meals, and using smoothies to help you control your weight or meet dietary requirements. We also stress the significance of paying attention to your body and customizing smoothie recipes to match your unique preferences and objectives.

CHAPTER 2: NUTRIBULLET BASICS: GETTING STARTED

This book is a thorough introduction to using your Nutribullet blender. This chapter includes the vital equipment, methods, and advice that will enable you to get the most out of your Nutribullet and prepare tasty smoothies that are also nourishing.

Unpacking and Getting to Know Your NutriBullet: We offer a detailed instruction manual for unpacking and assembling your Nutribullet blender. We describe each component, including the extractor blade, cups, lids, and motor base. To create a seamless and secure blending experience, we also go through safety considerations and proper handling.

Understanding the Extraction Method of the Nutribullet: It's critical to comprehend the Nutribullet's particular extraction procedure if you want to make the most of its potential. In this part, we look at how the Nutribullet's cyclonic movement and high-speed mixing break down fruits, vegetables, and other ingredients for the best possible nutritional extraction and texture. We also review how crucial blending methods and times are to getting the desired results.

Making Nutribullet Smoothies with the Best Ingredients: The appropriate components are the first step in making delicious and healthy smoothies. We recommend premium fruits, vegetables, leafy greens, nuts, seeds, and other ingredients. We talk about the value of seasonality, maturity, and freshness to maximize flavor and nutrient content. We also talk about organic, regional, and sustainable ingredient considerations.

Ingredient Preparation: Achieving smooth and reliable outcomes depends on adequately prepping your ingredients before blending. We go over how to wash, peel, and cut fruits and vegetables and pre-portioning and freezing advice to make the blending process go more quickly. We also offer advice on how to combine ingredients for well-balanced flavor and nutrient profiles.

Nutribullet Blending Methods and Speed Settings: You may adjust your Nutribullet's speed settings and blending methods to create smoothies that are unique to your tastes. We describe the various speed settings on the Nutribullet blender and suggest additional ingredients and preferred textures. We also review how to ensure even blending and avoid overheating by pulsing, pausing, and shaking.

NutriBullet Enhancements and Accessories: The section on Nutribullet accessories and improvements look at further add-ons and enhancements that can make blending using the appliance more enjoyable. We go over the accessories available to increase the functionality of your Nutribullet, from additional cups and lids for portability to specialty blades for milling grains or grinding nuts. We also use recipe books, apps, and online tools for inspiration and direction.

Cleaning and Maintaining Your Nutribullet: Your Nutribullet's longevity and peak performance depends on proper cleaning and maintenance. You can find detailed instructions for cleaning the cups, blades, and motor base of your Nutribullet here. We also advise removing harsh residue and avoiding odor or stain buildup. We also undergo routine maintenance procedures to keep your Nutribullet in good condition.

Tips and precautions for safety: It is crucial to ensure your safety while using the Nutribullet. We offer essential safety advice and safeguards, such as securing the cups and blades, preventing filling the cups to the brim, and never using damp hands to operate the blender. We also cover electrical safety, cord management, and suitable storage techniques to reduce potential concerns.

CHAPTER 3: CLASSIC FRUIT SMOOTHIE RECIPES

BERRY BLAST SMOOTHIE

Ingredients:

- 1 cup mixed berries (strawberries, blueberries, raspberries)
- One ripe banana
- 1/2 cup Greek yogurt
- 1/2 cup almond milk
- One tablespoon honey (optional)

Instructions:

1. Fill a blender with all the ingredients.
2. Blend until creamy and smooth.
3. To increase sweetness, if required, add more honey.
4. Enjoy when serving chilled!

TROPICAL PARADISE SMOOTHIE

Ingredients:
- 1 cup pineapple chunks
- One ripe mango peeled and pitted
- 1 banana
- 1/2 cup coconut milk
- 1/2 cup orange juice
- 1/2 cup ice cubes

Instructions:
1. Fill a blender with all the ingredients.
2. Blend until creamy and smooth.
3. Adjust the consistency as desired if additional coconut milk or orange juice is required.
4. Pour into chilled glasses and serve.

MANGO TANGO SMOOTHIE

Ingredients:
- 1 ripe mango, peeled and pitted
- 1/2 cup orange juice
- 1/2 cup Greek yogurt
- 1/4 cup coconut water
- 1 tablespoon honey (optional)
- Ice cubes (optional)

Instructions:
1. Mango, orange juice, Greek yogurt, and coconut water blend in a blender.

2. Purée until fluid.
3. If desired, add honey after tasting the mixture.
4. Blend the smoothie again after adding some ice cubes if you want it to be colder.
5. Pour into glasses, then sip.

STRAWBERRY BANANA DELIGHT

Ingredients:
- 1 cup strawberries, hulled
- 1 ripe banana
- 1/2 cup milk (dairy or non-dairy)
- 1/2 cup Greek yogurt
- 1 tablespoon honey (optional)
- Ice cubes (optional)

Instructions:
1. Put the milk, Greek yogurt, strawberries, banana, and honey (if using) in a blender.
2. Blend until creamy and smooth.
3. Blend the smoothie again after adding some ice cubes if you want it to be colder.
4. Pour into glasses, then offer.

BLUEBERRY POWER SMOOTHIE:

Ingredients:
- 1 cup blueberries
- 1 ripe banana

- 1/2 cup spinach leaves
- 1/2 cup almond milk
- 1/4 cup Greek yogurt
- 1 tablespoon chia seeds (optional)

Instructions:
1. Fill a blender with all the ingredients.
2. Blend until thoroughly integrated and smooth.
3. Add chia seeds for an additional nutritious boost, if preferred.
4. Pour into cups, then take a sip.

PEACHY KEEN SMOOTHIE

Ingredients:
- 2 ripe peaches, pitted and chopped
- 1/2 cup pineapple chunks
- 1/2 cup orange juice
- 1/2 cup plain yogurt
- 1/2 cup ice cubes
- 1 tablespoon honey (optional)

Instructions:
1. Fill a blender with peaches, pineapple chunks, orange juice, plain yogurt, ice cubes, and optional honey.
2. Blend until creamy and smooth.
3. Taste, and if necessary, add additional honey to balance the sweetness.
4. Pour into chilled glasses and serve.

WATERMELON REFRESHER

Ingredients:

- 2 cups cubed watermelon
- 1 cup cucumber, peeled and chopped
- 1/2 cup fresh mint leaves
- 1 tablespoon lime juice
- 1 tablespoon honey (optional)
- Ice cubes (optional)

Instructions:

1. Cubed watermelon, cucumber, fresh mint, lime juice, and honey (if desired) should all be combined in a blender.
2. Blend until thoroughly integrated and smooth.
3. Taste, and if necessary, add additional honey to balance the sweetness.
4. For a cold and refreshing texture, if preferred, add ice cubes.
5. After pouring, serve in glasses.

CITRUS SUNRISE SMOOTHIE

Ingredients:

- 1 orange, peeled and segmented
- 1 grapefruit, peeled and segmented
- 1 ripe banana
- 1/2 cup Greek yogurt
- 1/4 cup orange juice
- 1 tablespoon honey (optional)

- Ice cubes (optional)

Instructions:

1. Combine the orange and grapefruit segments, banana, Greek yogurt, orange juice, and any more honey you like in a blender.
2. Blend until creamy and smooth.
3. Add ice cubes and blend once more if you want an excellent smoothie.
4. Pour into glasses and savor the zesty scents of citrus.

PINEAPPLE PASSION SMOOTHIE

Ingredients:

- 1 cup pineapple chunks
- 1 passion fruit, pulp scooped out
- 1 banana
- 1/2 cup coconut milk
- 1/4 cup orange juice
- 1 tablespoon honey (optional)
- Ice cubes (optional)

Instructions:

1. In a blender, combine the chunks of pineapple, banana, coconut milk, orange juice, and honey (if using).
2. Blend until thoroughly integrated and smooth.
3. For a cooler and thicker consistency, if desired, add ice cubes.
4. Pour into glasses, then offer.

MIXED BERRY ANTIOXIDANT SMOOTHIE

Ingredients:

- 1 cup mixed berries (strawberries, blueberries, raspberries)
- 1/2 cup pomegranate juice
- 1/2 cup almond milk
- 1/2 cup Greek yogurt
- 1 tablespoon honey (optional)
- Ice cubes (optional)

Instructions:

1. Fill a blender with mixed berries, Greek yogurt, almond milk, pomegranate juice, and optional honey.
2. Blend until creamy and smooth.
3. For a cold and refreshing texture, if preferred, add ice cubes.
4. Pour the antioxidant-rich smoothie into glasses and savor it.

KIWI BERRY BLAST

Ingredients:

- 2 kiwis, peeled and chopped
- 1 cup mixed berries (strawberries, blueberries, raspberries)
- 1 cup spinach leaves
- 1 cup coconut water
- 1 tablespoon honey (optional)

- Ice cubes (optional)

Instructions:
1. Fill a blender with the kiwis, mixed berries, spinach leaves, coconut water, and honey (if using).
2. Blend until thoroughly integrated and smooth.
3. For a cooler and thicker consistency, if desired, add ice cubes.
4. Pour into cups, then take a sip.

RASPBERRY LEMONADE SMOOTHIE

Ingredients:
- 1 cup raspberries
- 1 ripe banana
- 1 tablespoon fresh lemon juice
- 1 cup almond milk
- 1 tablespoon honey (optional)
- Ice cubes (optional)

Instructions:
1. Fill a blender with the raspberries, banana, almond milk, fresh lemon juice, and honey (if using).
2. Blend until creamy and smooth.
3. Blend again after adding ice cubes for a more excellent smoothie.
4. Pour into glasses, then offer.

APPLE PIE SMOOTHIE

Ingredients:

- 1 apple, cored and chopped
- 1 ripe banana
- 1/2 cup rolled oats
- 1 cup almond milk
- 1 tablespoon honey or maple syrup
- 1/2 teaspoon cinnamon
- Ice cubes (optional)

Instructions:

1. Fill a blender halfway with the apple, banana, rolled oats, almond milk, honey or maple syrup, and cinnamon.
2. Blend until creamy and smooth.
3. If preferred, add ice cubes and mix one more.
4. Pour into glasses, add a dash of cinnamon, and sip.

PINA COLADA SMOOTHIE

Ingredients:

- 1 cup frozen pineapple chunks
- 1 ripe banana
- 1/2 cup coconut milk
- 1/2 cup pineapple juice
- 1/4 cup Greek yogurt
- 1 tablespoon honey or agave syrup
- Ice cubes (optional)

Instructions:

1. Combine the frozen pineapple chunks, banana, Greek yogurt, coconut milk, juice, and honey or agave syrup in a blender.
2. Blend until creamy and smooth.
3. If preferred, add ice cubes and mix one more.
4. Pour into glasses, add a pineapple wedge as a garnish, and serve.

ORANGE CREAMSICLE SMOOTHIE

Ingredients:

- 2 oranges, peeled and segmented
- 1 ripe banana
- 1/2 cup Greek yogurt
- 1/2 cup almond milk
- 1 tablespoon honey or maple syrup
- 1/2 teaspoon vanilla extract
- Ice cubes (optional)

Instructions:

1. Combine the banana, orange segments, Greek yogurt, almond milk, honey or maple syrup, and vanilla extract in a blender.
2. Blend until creamy and smooth.
3. If preferred, add ice cubes and mix one more.
4. Pour the energizing creamsicle flavor into glasses and savor.

GRAPEFRUIT GINGER ZING

Ingredients:

- 1 grapefruit, peeled and segmented
- 1-inch piece of fresh ginger, peeled and grated
- 1 ripe banana
- 1/2 cup coconut water
- 1 tablespoon honey or agave syrup
- Ice cubes (optional)

Instructions:

1. In a blender, combine the grapefruit segments, ginger that has been shredded, banana, coconut water, and honey or agave syrup.
2. Blend until thoroughly integrated and smooth.
3. If preferred, add ice cubes and mix one more.
4. Pour into glasses, garnish with a grapefruit slice or some grated ginger, and serve.

CHERRY VANILLA SMOOTHIE

Ingredients:

- 1 cup frozen cherries
- 1 ripe banana
- 1/2 cup Greek yogurt
- 1/2 cup almond milk
- 1 tablespoon honey or maple syrup
- 1/2 teaspoon vanilla extract
- Ice cubes (optional)

Instructions:

1. Combine Greek yogurt, banana, frozen cherries, honey or maple syrup, and vanilla extract in a blender.
2. Blend until creamy and smooth.
3. If preferred, add ice cubes and mix one more.
4. Pour the cherry vanilla delight into glasses and sip.

MELON MEDLEY SMOOTHIE

Ingredients:

- 1 cup diced mixed melons (watermelon, cantaloupe, honeydew)
- 1 ripe banana
- 1/2 cup coconut water
- 1/2 cup orange juice
- 1 tablespoon honey or agave syrup
- Ice cubes (optional)

Instructions:

1. Fill a blender halfway with the chopped mixed melon, banana, coconut water, orange juice, and honey or agave syrup.
2. Blend until thoroughly integrated and smooth.
3. For a cooler and thicker consistency, if desired, add ice cubes.
4. Pour into glasses, then offer.

PAPAYA PARADISE SMOOTHIE

Ingredients:

- 1 cup diced papaya
- 1 ripe banana
- 1/2 cup pineapple chunks
- 1/2 cup coconut milk
- 1/4 cup orange juice
- 1 tablespoon honey or agave syrup
- Ice cubes (optional)

Instructions:

1. Fill a blender with the diced papaya, banana, pineapple chunks, coconut milk, orange juice, and honey or agave syrup.
2. Blend until creamy and smooth.
3. If preferred, add ice cubes and mix one more.
4. Pour into glasses, if preferred, garnish with a papaya slice, and savor.

GUAVA GOODNESS SMOOTHIE

Ingredients:

- 1 cup guava chunks
- 1 ripe banana
- 1/2 cup Greek yogurt
- 1/2 cup coconut water
- 1 tablespoon honey or agave syrup
- Ice cubes (optional)

Instructions:

1. Place the banana, Greek yogurt, coconut water, honey, or agave syrup in a blender along with the guava chunks.
2. Blend until thoroughly integrated and smooth.
3. For a cooler and thicker consistency, if desired, add ice cubes.
4. Pour into glasses and enjoy the delicious guava flavor.

CHAPTER 4: GREEN AND VEGETABLE-PACKED SMOOTHIES

SPINACH AVOCADO POWER SMOOTHIE

Ingredients:

- 1 cup spinach leaves
- 1 ripe avocado
- 1 ripe banana
- 1 cup almond milk
- 1 tablespoon honey or maple syrup
- 1 tablespoon chia seeds (optional)
- Ice cubes (optional)

Instructions:

1. In a blender, combine the spinach leaves, avocado, banana, almond milk, honey or maple syrup, and chia seeds (if using).
2. Blend until creamy and smooth.
3. For a cooler and thicker consistency, if desired, add ice cubes.
4. Pour the rich green smoothie into glasses and sip.

KALE PINEAPPLE GREEN SMOOTHIE

Ingredients:

- 2 cups kale leaves, stems removed
- 1 cup frozen pineapple chunks

- 1 ripe banana
- 1 cup coconut water
- 1 tablespoon lime juice
- 1 tablespoon honey or agave syrup
- Ice cubes (optional)

Instructions:

1. Fill a blender with the kale leaves, banana, pineapple pieces, coconut water, lime juice, and honey or agave syrup.
2. Blend until thoroughly integrated and smooth.
3. For a cold and refreshing texture, if preferred, add ice cubes.
4. Pour the smoothie into glasses and sip on it.

GREEN DETOX SMOOTHIE

Ingredients:

- 1 cup spinach leaves
- 1 cucumber, peeled and chopped
- 1 green apple, cored and chopped
- 1 tablespoon fresh lemon juice
- 1 tablespoon grated ginger
- 1 cup coconut water
- Ice cubes (optional)

Instructions:

1. In a blender, combine the spinach leaves, cucumber, green apple, lemon juice, ginger that has been shredded, and coconut water.
2. Blend until thoroughly integrated and smooth.

3. If preferred, add ice cubes and mix one more.
4. Pour the cleansing green smoothie into glasses and sip.

CUCUMBER MINT COOLER

Ingredients:
- 1 cucumber, peeled and chopped
- 1/2 cup fresh mint leaves
- 1 tablespoon fresh lime juice
- 1 tablespoon honey or agave syrup
- 1 cup coconut water
- Ice cubes (optional)

Instructions:
1. Fill a blender with coconut water, lime juice, honey or agave syrup, cucumber, and fresh mint leaves.
2. Blend until thoroughly integrated and smooth.
3. For a cold and refreshing texture, if preferred, add ice cubes.
4. Pour the refreshing cucumber mint cooler into glasses, top with a mint sprig, and sip.

ZESTY BEET AND CARROT SMOOTHIE

Ingredients:
- 1 small beet, peeled and chopped
- 2 carrots, peeled and chopped
- 1 orange, peeled and segmented
- 1-inch piece of fresh ginger peeled

- 1 tablespoon honey or agave syrup
- 1 cup coconut water
- Ice cubes (optional)

Instructions:

1. Add the coconut water, honey or agave syrup, diced carrots, orange segments, fresh ginger, and beets to a blender.
2. Blend until thoroughly integrated and smooth.
3. If preferred, add ice cubes and mix one more.
4. Pour the tangy beet and carrot smoothie into glasses and savor.

BROCCOLI BLAST SMOOTHIE

Ingredients:

- 1 cup broccoli florets
- 1 ripe banana
- 1 cup almond milk
- 1 tablespoon honey or maple syrup
- 1 tablespoon chia seeds (optional)
- Ice cubes (optional)

Instructions:

1. Fill a blender with the broccoli florets, banana, almond milk, honey, maple syrup, and (if preferred) chia seeds.
2. Blend until creamy and smooth.
3. For a cooler and thicker consistency, if desired, add ice cubes.
4. Pour the wholesome broccoli blast smoothie into glasses and sip.

GREEN GODDESS SMOOTHIE

Ingredients:

- 2 cups spinach leaves
- 1 ripe avocado
- 1 green apple, cored and chopped
- 1/2 cup Greek yogurt
- 1 tablespoon honey or agave syrup
- 1 cup almond milk
- Ice cubes (optional)

Instructions:

1. Combine the spinach leaves, avocado, green apple, Greek yogurt, honey, or agave syrup in a blender.
2. Blend until thoroughly integrated and smooth.
3. If preferred, add ice cubes and mix one more.
4. Pour into glasses and enjoy the smoothie's healthy green flavor.

CELERY CUCUMBER REFRESHER

Ingredients:

- 2 stalks of celery, chopped
- 1 cucumber, peeled and chopped
- 1 green apple, cored and chopped
- 1 tablespoon fresh lemon juice
- 1 cup coconut water
- Ice cubes (optional)

Instructions:

1. Fill a blender halfway with celery, cucumber, green apple, lemon juice, and coconut water.
2. Blend until thoroughly integrated and smooth.
3. For a cold and refreshing texture, if preferred, add ice cubes.
4. Pour the hydrating and revitalizing celery cucumber refresher into glasses and sip.

ANTIOXIDANT GREEN SMOOTHIE

Ingredients:

- 2 cups kale leaves, stems removed
- 1 cup spinach leaves
- 1 cup frozen mixed berries (strawberries, blueberries, raspberries)
- 1 ripe banana
- 1 cup almond milk
- 1 tablespoon honey or maple syrup
- Ice cubes (optional)

Instructions:

1. Add the banana, almond milk, honey or maple syrup, frozen mixed berries, kale, spinach, and these ingredients to a blender.
2. Blend until thoroughly integrated and smooth.
3. For a cooler and thicker consistency, if desired, add ice cubes.
4. Pour the antioxidant-rich green smoothie into glasses and sip.

PEA PROTEIN GREEN SMOOTHIE

Ingredients:

- 1 cup spinach leaves
- 1 ripe banana
- 1 scoop pea protein powder
- 1 cup almond milk
- 1 tablespoon almond butter
- 1 tablespoon honey or maple syrup
- Ice cubes (optional)

Instructions:

1. Fill a blender with the spinach leaves, banana, pea protein powder, almond milk, almond butter, honey, or maple syrup.
2. Blend until creamy and smooth.
3. For a cooler and thicker consistency, if desired, add ice cubes.
4. Pour the protein-rich green smoothie into glasses and sip.

GARDEN GREENS SMOOTHIE

Ingredients:

- 2 cups mixed greens (spinach, kale, chard)
- 1 ripe banana
- 1 green apple, cored and chopped
- 1 cup almond milk
- 1 tablespoon honey or maple syrup
- Ice cubes (optional)

Instructions:

1. Fill a blender with the mixed greens, banana, green apple, almond milk, honey, and maple syrup.
2. Blend until thoroughly integrated and smooth.
3. For a cooler and thicker consistency, if desired, add ice cubes.
4. Pour the green smoothie into glasses and savor its garden-fresh flavor.

ZUCCHINI LIME SMOOTHIE

Ingredients:

- 1 medium zucchini, chopped
- Juice of 2 limes
- 1 ripe banana
- 1 cup coconut water
- 1 tablespoon honey or agave syrup
- Ice cubes (optional)

Instructions:

1. Fill a blender with the diced zucchini, lime juice, banana, coconut water, honey, or agave syrup.
2. Blend until thoroughly integrated and smooth.
3. For a cold and refreshing texture, if preferred, add ice cubes.
4. Pour the zesty zucchini lime smoothie into glasses and enjoy.

MINTY GREEN DELIGHT

Ingredients:

- 2 cups baby spinach
- 1/2 cup fresh mint leaves
- 1 ripe banana
- 1 cup coconut water
- 1 tablespoon honey or agave syrup
- Ice cubes (optional)

Instructions:

1. Combine the baby spinach, mint leaves, coconut water, banana, and honey or agave nectar in a blender.
2. Blend until thoroughly integrated and smooth.
3. For a cold and refreshing texture, if preferred, add ice cubes.
4. Pour into glasses, decorate with a mint leaf, and savor the minty-green treat.

ASPARAGUS DETOX SMOOTHIE

Ingredients:

- 1 cup chopped asparagus
- 1 green apple, cored and chopped
- 1 cup cucumber, peeled and chopped
- 1 tablespoon fresh lemon juice
- 1 tablespoon grated ginger
- 1 cup coconut water
- Ice cubes (optional)

Instructions:

1. Fill a blender with the chopped asparagus, green apple, cucumber, grated ginger, lemon juice, and coconut water.
2. Blend until thoroughly integrated and smooth.
3. For a cold and refreshing texture, if preferred, add ice cubes.
4. Pour the cleansing smoothie of asparagus into glasses and savor.

GREEN APPLE GINGER SMOOTHIE

Ingredients:

- 1 green apple, cored and chopped
- 1 cup spinach leaves
- 1-inch piece of fresh ginger, peeled and grated
- 1 ripe banana
- 1 cup almond milk
- 1 tablespoon honey or maple syrup
- Ice cubes (optional)

Instructions:

1. In a blender, combine the green apple, spinach leaves, ginger that has been grated, banana, almond milk, and honey or maple syrup.
2. Blend until thoroughly integrated and smooth.
3. For a cold and refreshing texture, if preferred, add ice cubes.
4. Pour the refreshing green apple ginger smoothie into glasses and sip.

SWEET SPINACH MANGO SMOOTHIE

Ingredients:

- 2 cups baby spinach
- 1 ripe mango, peeled and chopped
- 1 ripe banana
- 1 cup coconut water
- 1 tablespoon honey or agave syrup
- Ice cubes (optional)

Instructions:

1. Combine the baby spinach, mango, banana, coconut water, and honey or agave nectar in a blender.
2. Blend until thoroughly integrated and smooth.
3. For a cold and refreshing texture, if preferred, add ice cubes.
4. Pour the delicious and wholesome spinach mango smoothie into glasses and sip.

PARSLEY PEAR POWER SMOOTHIE

Ingredients:

- 1 cup fresh parsley
- 1 ripe pear, cored and chopped
- 1/2 cup cucumber, peeled and chopped
- 1/2 cup coconut water
- Juice of 1 lemon
- 1 tablespoon honey or agave syrup
- Ice cubes (optional)

Instructions:

1. Combine the fresh parsley, pear, cucumber chunks, coconut water, lemon juice, and honey or agave syrup in a blender.
2. Blend until thoroughly integrated and smooth.
3. For a cold and refreshing texture, if preferred, add ice cubes.
4. Pour the nutritious parsley-pear smoothie into glasses and sip on it.

CABBAGE LIME CLEANSER

Ingredients:

- 2 cups shredded green cabbage
- Juice of 2 limes
- 1 ripe banana
- 1 cup coconut water
- 1 tablespoon honey or agave syrup
- Ice cubes (optional)

Instructions:

1. In a blender, combine the lime juice, banana, coconut water, honey, or agave syrup, and the green cabbage that has been shredded.
2. Blend until thoroughly integrated and smooth.
3. For a cold and refreshing texture, if preferred, add ice cubes.
4. Pour into glasses and savor the cabbage lime cleanser's purifying abilities.

BRUSSELS SPROUT BERRY BLEND

Ingredients:

- 1 cup steamed Brussels sprouts
- 1 cup mixed berries (strawberries, blueberries, raspberries)
- 1 ripe banana
- 1 cup almond milk
- 1 tablespoon honey or agave syrup
- Ice cubes (optional)

Instructions:

1. Fill a blender with the banana, almond milk, honey or agave syrup, mixed berries, steaming Brussels sprouts, and almonds.
2. Blend until thoroughly integrated and smooth.
3. For a cold and refreshing texture, if preferred, add ice cubes.
4. Pour into glasses and savor the delicious union of berries and Brussels sprouts.

GREEN KIWI KALE SMOOTHIE

Ingredients:

- 2 kiwis, peeled and chopped
- 1 cup kale leaves, stems removed
- 1 ripe banana
- 1 cup coconut water
- 1 tablespoon honey or agave syrup

- Ice cubes (optional)

Instructions:

1. Fill a blender with the diced kiwis, kale, banana, coconut water, honey, and agave syrup.
2. Blend until thoroughly integrated and smooth.
3. For a cold and refreshing texture, if preferred, add ice cubes.
4. Pour the brilliant green kiwi kale smoothie into glasses and savor it.

CHAPTER 5: PROTEIN-POWERED SMOOTHIE CREATIONS

CHOCOLATE BANANA PROTEIN SHAKE

Ingredients:

- 1 ripe banana
- 1 scoop of chocolate protein powder
- 1 cup milk (dairy or non-dairy)
- 1 tablespoon almond butter
- 1 tablespoon cocoa powder
- Ice cubes (optional)

Instructions:

1. Fill a blender with the ripe banana, milk, almond butter, cocoa powder, and ice cubes (if preferred). Blend until smooth.
2. Blend until thoroughly integrated and smooth.

3. Add more milk or ice cubes if you like a thinner or thicker texture.
4. Pour the protein shake into a glass and savor its chocolatey sweetness.

VANILLA ALMOND PROTEIN SMOOTHIE

Ingredients:

- 1 cup almond milk
- 1 scoop vanilla protein powder
- 1 ripe banana
- 1 tablespoon almond butter
- 1 teaspoon honey or maple syrup
- Ice cubes (optional)

Instructions:

1. Fill a blender with the almond milk, vanilla protein powder, banana that has reached peak ripeness, almond butter, honey or maple syrup, and (if wanted) ice cubes.
2. Blend until thoroughly integrated and smooth.
3. If necessary, increase the honey or maple syrup to adjust the sweetness.
4. Pour the creamy and nutty vanilla almond protein smoothie into a glass and savor it.

PEANUT BUTTER CHOCOLATE PROTEIN BLAST

Ingredients:

- 1 cup milk (dairy or non-dairy)
- 1 scoop of chocolate protein powder
- 2 tablespoons peanut butter
- 1 ripe banana
- 1 tablespoon cocoa powder
- Ice cubes (optional)

Instructions:

1. Combine the milk, chocolate protein powder, peanut butter, ripe banana, cocoa powder, and any optional ice cubes in a blender.
2. Blend until thoroughly integrated and smooth.
3. Add more milk or ice cubes if you like a thinner or thicker texture.
4. Pour the delicious and filling peanut butter chocolate protein blitz into a glass.

BERRY PROTEIN POWER SMOOTHIE

Ingredients:

- 1 cup mixed berries (strawberries, blueberries, raspberries)
- 1 scoop vanilla protein powder
- 1 cup almond milk
- 1 ripe banana

- 1 tablespoon honey or agave syrup
- Ice cubes (optional)

Instructions:

1. Fill a blender with the mixed berries, almond milk, ripe banana, honey or agave syrup, and ice cubes (if desired).
2. Blend until thoroughly integrated and smooth.
3. If necessary, increase the honey or agave syrup to adjust the sweetness.
4. Pour the tasty, protein-rich berry smoothie into a glass and savor it.

COFFEE PROTEIN SHAKE

Ingredients:

- 1 cup brewed coffee, cooled
- 1 scoop of chocolate protein powder
- 1 cup milk (dairy or non-dairy)
- 1 ripe banana
- 1 tablespoon almond butter
- Ice cubes (optional)

Instructions:

1. Combine the brewed coffee, milk, ripe banana, almond butter, and ice cubes (if desired) in a blender.
2. Blend until thoroughly integrated and smooth.
3. Change the consistency by adding more ice cubes for a thicker texture or milk for a thinner shake.
4. Pour the invigorating coffee protein shake into a glass and sip.

GREEN PROTEIN BOOST SMOOTHIE

Ingredients:

- 1 cup spinach leaves
- 1 scoop vanilla protein powder
- 1 cup almond milk
- 1 ripe banana
- 1 tablespoon almond butter
- 1 tablespoon honey or maple syrup
- Ice cubes (optional)

Instructions:

1. Combine the spinach leaves, vanilla protein powder, almond milk, ripe banana, almond butter, honey, maple syrup, and whatever ice cubes you like in a blender.
2. Blend until thoroughly integrated and smooth.
3. If necessary, increase the honey or maple syrup to adjust the sweetness.
4. Pour the healthful, protein-rich green smoothie into a glass and sip.

TROPICAL MANGO PROTEIN SMOOTHIE

Ingredients:

- 1 cup frozen mango chunks
- 1 scoop vanilla protein powder
- 1 cup coconut milk
- 1 ripe banana
- 1 tablespoon shredded coconut

- Ice cubes (optional)

Instructions:

1. Fill a blender with the coconut milk, ripe banana, shredded coconut, vanilla protein powder, frozen mango chunks, and ice cubes (if preferred).
2. Blend until thoroughly integrated and smooth.
3. Change the consistency by adding more ice cubes for a thicker texture or more coconut milk for a thinner smoothie.
4. Pour into a glass and savor the mango protein smoothie's, tropical sweetness.

CHOCOLATE MINT PROTEIN SHAKE

Ingredients:

- 1 cup milk (dairy or non-dairy)
- 1 scoop of chocolate protein powder
- 1 tablespoon cocoa powder
- 1 tablespoon fresh mint leaves
- 1 ripe banana
- Ice cubes (optional)

Instructions:

1. In a blender, combine the milk, chocolate protein powder, cocoa powder, mint leaves that have just been picked, ripe banana, and ice cubes (if preferred).
2. Blend until thoroughly integrated and smooth.
3. Adjust the sweetness by incorporating additional cocoa powder or a preferred sweetener if necessary.

4. Pour the energizing chocolate mint protein shake into a glass and sip.

CHERRY ALMOND PROTEIN SMOOTHIE

Ingredients:

- 1 cup frozen cherries
- 1 scoop vanilla protein powder
- 1 cup almond milk
- 1 ripe banana
- 1 tablespoon almond butter
- Ice cubes (optional)

Instructions:

1. Fill a blender with the almond milk, ripe banana, almond butter, vanilla protein powder, frozen cherries, and ice cubes (if desired).
2. Blend until thoroughly integrated and smooth.
3. Change the consistency by adding more ice cubes for a thicker texture or almond milk for a thinner smoothie.
4. Pour the tasty cherry almond protein smoothie into a glass and savor.

PUMPKIN SPICE PROTEIN SMOOTHIE

Ingredients:

- 1 cup pumpkin puree
- 1 scoop vanilla protein powder
- 1 cup almond milk

- 1 ripe banana
- 1 tablespoon honey or maple syrup
- 1/2 teaspoon pumpkin spice
- Ice cubes (optional)

Instructions:

1. Fill a blender with the pumpkin puree, vanilla protein powder, almond milk, ripe banana, honey or maple syrup, pumpkin spice, and (if preferred) ice cubes.
2. Blend until thoroughly integrated and smooth.
3. Tailor the amount of sweetness and spice to your tastes.
4. Pour into a glass and savor the pumpkin spice protein smoothie, a festive treat.

STRAWBERRY PROTEIN DELIGHT

Ingredients:

- 1 cup frozen strawberries
- 1 scoop strawberry protein powder
- 1 cup almond milk
- 1 ripe banana
- 1 tablespoon honey or agave syrup
- Ice cubes (optional)

Instructions:

1. Fill a blender with almond milk, ripe banana, honey or agave syrup, frozen strawberries, strawberry protein powder, and ice cubes (if desired).
2. Blend until thoroughly integrated and smooth.
3. If necessary, increase the honey or agave syrup to adjust the sweetness.

4. Pour the delicious strawberry protein smoothie into a glass and sip.

BLUEBERRY PROTEIN BLAST

Ingredients:

- 1 cup frozen blueberries
- 1 scoop vanilla protein powder
- 1 cup almond milk
- 1 ripe banana
- 1 tablespoon almond butter
- Ice cubes (optional)

Instructions:

1. Fill a blender with the almond milk, ripe banana, almond butter, vanilla protein powder, frozen blueberries, and ice cubes (if desired).
2. Blend until thoroughly integrated and smooth.
3. Change the consistency by adding more ice cubes for a thicker texture or almond milk for a thinner smoothie.
4. Pour the berry-filled protein blitz into a glass and sip.

CINNAMON ROLL PROTEIN SHAKE

Ingredients:

- 1 cup milk (dairy or non-dairy)
- 1 scoop vanilla protein powder
- 1 ripe banana
- 1 tablespoon almond butter

- 1 teaspoon cinnamon
- 1/2 teaspoon vanilla extract
- Ice cubes (optional)

Instructions:

1. In a blender, combine the milk, vanilla protein powder, banana that has reached peak ripeness, almond butter, cinnamon, vanilla extract, and any ice cubes you like.
2. Blend until thoroughly integrated and smooth.
3. Tailor the amount of sweetness and spice to your tastes.
4. Pour the protein smoothie inspired by cinnamon rolls into a glass and savor.

PEACHY PROTEIN SMOOTHIE

Ingredients:

- 1 cup frozen peaches
- 1 scoop vanilla protein powder
- 1 cup almond milk
- 1 ripe banana
- 1 tablespoon honey or agave syrup
- Ice cubes (optional)

Instructions:

1. Fill a blender with almond milk, ripe banana, honey or agave syrup, vanilla protein powder, frozen peaches, and ice cubes (if desired).
2. Blend until thoroughly integrated and smooth.
3. If necessary, increase the honey or agave syrup to adjust the sweetness.
4. Pour the peachy protein smoothie into a glass and sip.

MOCHA PROTEIN FRAPPE

Ingredients:

- 1 cup cold brewed coffee
- 1 scoop of chocolate protein powder
- 1 cup almond milk
- 1 tablespoon almond butter
- 1 tablespoon cocoa powder
- Ice cubes (optional)

Instructions:

1. Combine the cold-brewed coffee, chocolate protein powder, almond milk, almond butter, cocoa powder, and any additional ice you like in a blender.
2. Blend until thoroughly integrated and smooth.
3. Change the consistency by adding more ice cubes for a thicker texture or almond milk for a thinner frappe.
4. Pour the refreshing mocha protein frappe into a glass and sip.

CHOCOLATE PEANUT BUTTER BANANA SMOOTHIE

1. Ingredients:

- 1 ripe banana
- 1 scoop of chocolate protein powder
- 1 tablespoon peanut butter
- 1 cup almond milk
- 1 tablespoon cocoa powder
- Ice cubes (optional)

Instructions:
2. Place the ripe banana in a blender with the chocolate protein powder, peanut butter, almond milk, cocoa powder, and ice cubes (if preferred).
3. Blend until thoroughly integrated and smooth.
4. Adjust the sweetness by incorporating additional cocoa powder or a preferred sweetener if necessary.
5. Pour the luscious chocolate peanut butter banana smoothie into a glass and savor.

COOKIES AND CREAM PROTEIN SHAKE

Ingredients:

- 1 cup milk (dairy or non-dairy)
- 1 scoop of cookies and cream protein powder
- 1 ripe banana
- 2-3 chocolate sandwich cookies
- Ice cubes (optional)

Instructions:

1. Combine the milk, cookies, cream protein powder, ripe banana, chocolate sandwich cookies, and any additional ice cubes you like in a blender.
2. Blend until thoroughly integrated and smooth.
3. Change the consistency by adding more ice cubes for a thicker texture or milk for a thinner shake.
4. Pour the decadent cookies and cream protein smoothie into a glass and sip.

PEANUT BUTTER BANANA BERRY PROTEIN SMOOTHIE

Ingredients:

- 1 ripe banana
- 1 scoop mixed berry protein powder
- 1 tablespoon peanut butter
- 1 cup almond milk
- 1/2 cup mixed berries (strawberries, blueberries, raspberries)

- Ice cubes (optional)

Instructions:

1. Fill a blender with the ripe banana, protein powder made from mixed berries, peanut butter, almond milk, mixed berries, and ice cubes (if preferred).
2. Blend until thoroughly integrated and smooth.
3. Adjust the sweetness by including more berries or a different sweetener if necessary.
4. Pour the protein smoothie into a glass and savor the flavorful fusion of peanut butter, banana, and berries.

MATCHA PROTEIN POWERHOUSE

- Ingredients:
- 1 cup almond milk
- 1 scoop vanilla protein powder
- 1 teaspoon matcha powder
- 1 ripe banana
- 1 tablespoon honey or agave syrup
- Ice cubes (optional)

Instructions:

1. Fill a blender with the almond milk, vanilla protein powder, matcha powder, banana that has reached peak ripeness, honey or agave syrup, and ice cubes (if desired).
2. Blend until thoroughly integrated and smooth.
3. Tailor the matcha flavor and sweetness to your tastes.
4. Pour the vivid and invigorating matcha protein powerhouse into a glass and enjoy.

COCONUT CHOCOLATE PROTEIN SHAKE

Ingredients:

- 1 cup coconut milk
- 1 scoop of chocolate protein powder
- 1 tablespoon coconut flakes
- 1 ripe banana
- 1 tablespoon almond butter
- Ice cubes (optional)

Instructions:

1. In a blender, combine the coconut milk, chocolate protein powder, coconut flakes, banana that has reached peak ripeness, almond butter, and ice cubes (if using).
2. Blend until thoroughly integrated and smooth.
3. Tailor the sweetness and flavor of the coconut to your tastes.
4. Pour into a glass and savor the coconut chocolate protein shake with a touch of the tropics.

CREAMY COCONUT BERRY SMOOTHIE

Ingredients:

- 1 cup coconut milk
- 1 cup mixed berries (strawberries, blueberries, raspberries)
- 1 banana
- 1 tablespoon honey (optional)
- ½ cup ice cubes

Instructions:

1. Blend the items in a blender.
2. Blend till smooth and creamy at high speed.
3. To serve, pour into a glass.

ALMOND BUTTER BANANA SMOOTHIE

Ingredients:

- 1 cup almond milk
- 1 banana
- 2 tablespoons almond butter
- 1 tablespoon honey (optional)
- ½ teaspoon vanilla extract
- ½ cup ice cubes

Instructions:
1. To a blender, add all the ingredients.
2. Blend till creamy and smooth.
3. Place in a glass and sip.

CHIA SEED PUDDING SMOOTHIE

Ingredients:
- 1 cup almond milk
- 2 tablespoons chia seeds
- 1 tablespoon honey or maple syrup
- ½ teaspoon vanilla extract
- 1 banana
- ½ cup frozen berries
- ½ cup ice cubes

Instructions:
1. Combine the chia seeds, almond milk, honey or maple syrup, and vanilla extract in a dish. Stir thoroughly and allow the chia seeds to absorb the liquid for 10 minutes or until they resemble pudding.
2. Pour the chia seed pudding ingredients into a blender.
3. Fill the blender with the ice cubes, frozen berries, and banana.
4. Blend until creamy and smooth.
5. Transfer to a glass and serve.

MANGO COCONUT MILK SMOOTHIE

Ingredients:

- 1 cup coconut milk
- 1 ripe mango, peeled and pitted
- 1 banana
- 1 tablespoon honey (optional)
- ½ cup ice cubes

Instructions:

1. Fill a blender with all the ingredients.
2. Blend until creamy and smooth.
3. Pour into a glass and savor the deliciousness of the tropics.

RASPBERRY CASHEW SMOOTHIE

Ingredients:

- 1 cup almond milk
- 1 cup raspberries
- ¼ cup cashews
- 1 tablespoon honey (optional)
- ½ teaspoon vanilla extract
- ½ cup ice cubes

Instructions:

1. Fill a blender with all the ingredients.
2. Blend until creamy and smooth.
3. Pour the mixture into a glass to serve.

TURMERIC GOLDEN MILK SMOOTHIE

Ingredients:
- 1 cup coconut milk
- 1 banana
- 1 teaspoon turmeric powder
- ½ teaspoon cinnamon
- 1 tablespoon honey (optional)
- ½ teaspoon grated fresh ginger
- ½ cup ice cubes

Instructions:
1. Fill a blender with all the ingredients.
2. Blend until creamy and smooth.
3. Pour into a glass and take pleasure in turmeric's health advantages.

GREEN TEA MATCHA SMOOTHIE

Ingredients:
- 1 cup almond milk
- 1 teaspoon matcha green tea powder
- 1 banana
- 1 tablespoon honey (optional)
- ½ cup spinach leaves
- ½ cup ice cubes

Instructions:
1. Fill a blender with all the ingredients.
2. Blend until creamy and smooth.

3. Pour the mixture into a glass to serve.

AVOCADO LIME SMOOTHIE

Ingredients:
- 1 ripe avocado, peeled and pitted
- 1 cup coconut water
- Juice of 1 lime
- 1 tablespoon honey (optional)
- ½ cup ice cubes

Instructions:
1. Fill a blender with all the ingredients.
2. Blend until creamy and smooth.
3. Pour the fruity avocado and lime concoction into a glass and sip.

PINEAPPLE COCONUT WATER SMOOTHIE

Ingredients:
- 1 cup coconut water
- 1 cup frozen pineapple chunks
- 1 banana
- 1 tablespoon lime juice
- 1 tablespoon honey (optional)
- ½ cup ice cubes

Instructions:
1. Fill a blender with all the ingredients.

2. Blend until creamy and smooth.
3. Pour the mixture into a glass to serve.

OATMEAL COOKIE SMOOTHIE

Ingredients:

- 1 cup almond milk
- ½ cup rolled oats
- 1 banana
- 2 tablespoons almond butter
- 1 tablespoon honey (optional)
- 1 teaspoon vanilla extract
- ½ teaspoon ground cinnamon
- ½ cup ice cubes

Instructions:

1. Fill a blender with all the ingredients.
2. Blend until creamy and smooth.
3. Pour into a glass and savor the smoothie's version of the flavor of an oatmeal cookie.

CREAMY CHOCOLATE AVOCADO SMOOTHIE

Ingredients:

- 1 ripe avocado, peeled and pitted
- 1 cup almond milk
- 2 tablespoons cocoa powder
- 2 tablespoons honey or maple syrup

- ½ teaspoon vanilla extract
- ½ cup ice cubes

Instructions:

1. Fill a blender with all the ingredients.
2. Blend until creamy and smooth.
3. Pour the decadent chocolate avocado delight into a glass and savor.

SPIRULINA SUPERFOOD SMOOTHIE

Ingredients:

- 1 cup coconut water
- 1 banana
- 1 cup spinach leaves
- 1 tablespoon spirulina powder
- 1 tablespoon honey or maple syrup
- ½ cup ice cubes

Instructions:

1. Fill a blender with all the ingredients.
2. Blend until thoroughly integrated and smooth.
3. Pour the nutrient-dense superfood smoothie into a glass and sip.

BLUEBERRY ALMOND MILK SMOOTHIE

Ingredients:
- 1 cup almond milk
- 1 cup blueberries (fresh or frozen)
- 1 banana
- 1 tablespoon honey or maple syrup
- ½ teaspoon vanilla extract
- ½ cup ice cubes

Instructions:
1. Fill a blender with all the ingredients.
2. Blend until creamy and smooth.
3. Pour into a glass and enjoy the mouthwatering blueberry taste.

PAPAYA GINGER LIME SMOOTHIE

Ingredients:
- 1 cup coconut water
- 1 cup diced papaya
- Juice of 1 lime
- 1 tablespoon grated fresh ginger
- 1 tablespoon honey or maple syrup
- ½ cup ice cubes

Instructions:
1. Fill a blender with all the ingredients.
2. Blend until thoroughly integrated and smooth.

3. Pour into a glass, then savor the flavor of the tropical breeze.

CREAMY PUMPKIN SPICE SMOOTHIE

Ingredients:
- 1 cup almond milk
- ½ cup pumpkin puree
- 1 banana
- 1 tablespoon honey or maple syrup
- ½ teaspoon pumpkin spice mix (cinnamon, nutmeg, ginger, cloves)
- ½ cup ice cubes

Instructions:
1. Fill a blender with all the ingredients.
2. Blend until creamy and smooth.
3. Pour into a glass and enjoy the delicious pumpkin spice flavors.

COCONUT RASPBERRY BLISS SMOOTHIE

Ingredients:
- 1 cup coconut milk
- 1 cup raspberries (fresh or frozen)
- 1 banana
- 1 tablespoon honey or maple syrup
- ½ cup ice cubes

Instructions:

1. Fill a blender with all the ingredients.
2. Blend until thoroughly integrated and smooth.
3. Pour into a glass and savor the delicious berry and tropical flavors.

PEANUT BUTTER OAT SMOOTHIE

Ingredients:

- 1 cup almond milk
- 2 tablespoons peanut butter
- ¼ cup rolled oats
- 1 banana
- 1 tablespoon honey or maple syrup
- ½ teaspoon vanilla extract
- ½ cup ice cubes

Instructions:

1. Fill a blender with all the ingredients.
2. Blend until creamy and smooth.
3. Pour into a glass, then sip to enjoy the creamy and nutty flavors.

ALMOND JOY SMOOTHIE

Ingredients:

- 1 cup almond milk
- 2 tablespoons cocoa powder
- 2 tablespoons shredded coconut

- 1 tablespoon almond butter
- 1 tablespoon honey or maple syrup
- ½ teaspoon vanilla extract
- ½ cup ice cubes

Instructions:

1. Fill a blender with all the ingredients.
2. Blend until thoroughly integrated and smooth.
3. Pour into a glass, then savor the sweetness that tastes like an Almond Joy chocolate bar.

SPICED CARROT CAKE SMOOTHIE

Ingredients:

- 1 cup almond milk
- 1 cup grated carrots
- 1 banana
- 2 tablespoons rolled oats
- 1 tablespoon honey or maple syrup
- ½ teaspoon vanilla extract
- ½ teaspoon ground cinnamon
- ¼ teaspoon ground nutmeg
- ¼ teaspoon ground ginger
- ½ cup ice cubes

Instructions:

1. Fill a blender with all the ingredients.
2. Blend until thoroughly integrated and smooth.
3. Pour into a glass and savor the smoothie's rendition of the taste of a spiced carrot cake.

HAZELNUT MOCHA SMOOTHIE

Ingredients:

- 1 cup almond milk
- 1 ripe banana
- 2 tablespoons hazelnut butter or Nutella
- 1 tablespoon cocoa powder
- 1 tablespoon instant coffee or espresso powder
- 1 tablespoon honey or maple syrup
- ½ teaspoon vanilla extract
- ½ cup ice cubes

Instructions:

1. Fill a blender with all the ingredients.
2. Blend until creamy and smooth.
3. Pour the beverage into a glass and savor the decadent, creamy hazelnut mocha flavor.

PEANUT BUTTER BANANA CHOCOLATE SMOOTHIE

Ingredients:

- 1 ripe banana
- 2 tablespoons peanut butter
- 1 cup almond milk
- 2 tablespoons cocoa powder
- 1 tablespoon honey or sweetener of your choice (optional)
- Ice cubes (optional)

Instructions:

1. Cut the banana into chunks after peeling it.
2. Blend the banana chunks, almond milk, cocoa powder, and honey (if using) in a blender.
3. Puree everything until it's creamy and smooth.
4. Add some ice cubes and blend the smoothie until it is cold and foamy.
5. Pour into a glass, then take a sip.

ALMOND JOY CHOCOLATE SMOOTHIE

Ingredients:

- 1 ripe banana
- 2 tablespoons almond butter
- 1 cup coconut milk
- 2 tablespoons cocoa powder
- 2 tablespoons shredded coconut
- 1 tablespoon honey or sweetener of your choice (optional)
- Ice cubes (optional)

Instructions:

1. Cut the banana into chunks after peeling it.
2. Place the banana chunks, almond butter, coconut milk, cocoa powder, coconut shreds, and honey (if using) in a blender.
3. Puree everything until it's creamy and smooth.
4. Add some ice cubes and blend the smoothie until it is cold and foamy.
5. Pour into a glass, if preferred, top with additional coconut shreds, and enjoy!

HAZELNUT NUTELLA DELIGHT

Ingredients:

- 1 ripe banana
- 2 tablespoons Nutella or hazelnut spread
- 1 cup milk (dairy or plant-based)
- 1 tablespoon cocoa powder
- 1 tablespoon honey or sweetener of your choice (optional)
- Ice cubes (optional)

Instructions:

1. Cut the banana into chunks after peeling it.
2. Blend the banana chunks, milk, cocoa powder, honey (if using), Nutella or hazelnut spread, and other ingredients in a blender.
3. Puree everything until it's creamy and smooth.
4. Add some ice cubes and blend the smoothie until it is cold and foamy.
5. Pour the delightful hazelnut Nutella treat into a glass and enjoy!

CHOCOLATE COVERED STRAWBERRY SMOOTHIE

Ingredients:

- 1 cup strawberries (fresh or frozen)
- 1 cup milk (dairy or plant-based)
- 2 tablespoons cocoa powder
- 1 tablespoon honey or sweetener of your choice (optional)
- 1/2 teaspoon vanilla extract
- Ice cubes (optional)

Instructions:

1. Strawberry hulling and washing.
2. Place the milk, cocoa powder, vanilla extract, honey (if using), and strawberries in a blender.
3. Blend the ingredients until they are well combined and smooth.
4. Add some ice cubes and blend the smoothie until it is cold and foamy.
5. Pour into a glass, and if desired, top with a strawberry. Enjoy the delicious chocolate-covered strawberries!

CASHEW BUTTER AND DATE SMOOTHIE

Ingredients:

- 1 ripe banana
- 2 tablespoons cashew butter
- 2 dates pitted
- 1 cup almond milk
- 1 tablespoon honey or sweetener of your choice (optional)
- Ice cubes (optional)

Instructions:

1. Cut the banana into chunks after peeling it.
2. Blend the banana chunks, dates, cashew butter, almond milk, and honey (if using) in a blender.
3. Puree everything until it's creamy and smooth.
4. Add some ice cubes and blend the smoothie until it is cold and foamy.
5. Pour the nutty, sweet cashew butter and date smoothie into a glass and savor!

WHITE CHOCOLATE RASPBERRY SMOOTHIE

Ingredients:

- 1 cup frozen raspberries
- 1 cup milk (dairy or plant-based)
- 2 tablespoons white chocolate chips
- 1 tablespoon honey or sweetener of your choice (optional)
- 1/2 teaspoon vanilla extract
- Ice cubes (optional)

Instructions:

1. Combine the milk, white chocolate chips, vanilla extract, honey (if using), and frozen raspberries in a blender.
2. Purée everything until it's smooth and evenly distributed.
3. Add some ice cubes and reblend the smoothie until it is cold and foamy.
4. Pour the concoction of white chocolate and raspberries into a glass and enjoy!

MACADAMIA NUT CHOCOLATE SMOOTHIE

Ingredients:

- 1 ripe banana
- 2 tablespoons macadamia nut butter
- 1 cup coconut milk
- 2 tablespoons cocoa powder

- 1 tablespoon honey or sweetener of your choice (optional)
- Ice cubes (optional)

Instructions:

1. Cut the banana into chunks after peeling it.
2. Combine the fragments of banana, macadamia nut butter, coconut milk, cocoa powder, and honey (if using) in a blender.
3. Puree everything until it's creamy and smooth.
4. Add some ice cubes and blend the smoothie until it is cold and foamy.
5. Pour into a glass, and for an added crunch, you may top it with some crushed macadamia nuts. Enjoy the chocolate macadamia nut smoothie, which is rich and nutty.

SALTED CARAMEL PEANUT BUTTER SMOOTHIE

Ingredients:

- 1 ripe banana
- 2 tablespoons peanut butter
- 1 cup milk (dairy or plant-based)
- 1 tablespoon cocoa powder
- 1 tablespoon caramel sauce
- Pinch of sea salt
- Ice cubes (optional)

Instructions:

1. Cut the banana into chunks after peeling it.

2. Combine the banana chunks, peanut butter, milk, cocoa powder, caramel sauce, and a dash of salt in a blender.
3. Blend the ingredients until they are well combined and smooth.
4. Add some ice cubes and blend the smoothie until it is cold and foamy.
5. Pour the luscious salted peanut butter smoothie into a glass, add more caramel sauce to taste, and savor!

CHOCOLATE CHERRY ALMOND SMOOTHIE

Ingredients:
- 1 cup frozen cherries
- 1 cup almond milk
- 2 tablespoons almond butter
- 2 tablespoons cocoa powder
- 1 tablespoon honey or sweetener of your choice (optional)
- Ice cubes (optional)

Instructions:
1. The frozen cherries, almond milk, almond butter, cocoa powder, and honey (if used) should all be combined in a blender.
2. Purée everything until it's smooth and evenly distributed.
3. Add some ice cubes and reblend the smoothie until it is cold and foamy.
4. Pour into a glass and savor the delectable chocolate, cherry, and almond flavors!

NUTTY MOCHA SMOOTHIE

Ingredients:

- 1 ripe banana
- 2 tablespoons almond butter
- 1 cup brewed coffee, chilled
- 1 tablespoon cocoa powder
- 1 tablespoon honey or sweetener of your choice (optional)
- Ice cubes (optional)

Instructions:

1. Cut the banana into chunks after peeling it.
2. Banana chunks, almond butter, cooled brewed coffee, cocoa powder, and honey (if using) should all be combined in a blender.
3. Puree everything until it's creamy and smooth.
4. Add some ice cubes and blend the smoothie until it is cold and foamy.
5. Pour the energetic and decadent nutty mocha smoothie into a glass and savor!

PEANUT BUTTER CUP SMOOTHIE

Ingredients:

- 1 ripe banana
- 2 tablespoons peanut butter
- 1 cup milk (dairy or plant-based)
- 2 tablespoons cocoa powder

- 1 tablespoon honey or sweetener of your choice (optional)
- 1/4 cup crushed chocolate peanut butter cups
- Ice cubes (optional)

Instructions:

1. Cut the banana into chunks after peeling it.
2. Combine the banana chunks, milk, cocoa powder, and honey (if using) in a blender.
3. Puree everything until it's creamy and smooth.
4. Add some ice cubes and blend the smoothie until it is cold and foamy.
5. Add the broken chocolate peanut butter cups and stir.
6. If preferred, pour into a glass and add more crushed peanut butter cups as a garnish. Enjoy your smoothie with peanut butter cups!

CHOCOLATE MINT PROTEIN SMOOTHIE

Ingredients:

- 1 ripe banana
- 1 cup milk (dairy or plant-based)
- 2 tablespoons chocolate protein powder
- 1 tablespoon cocoa powder
- 1/4 teaspoon peppermint extract
- 1 tablespoon honey or sweetener of your choice (optional)
- Ice cubes (optional)
- Fresh mint leaves for garnish (optional)

Instructions:

1. Cut the banana into chunks after peeling it.
2. Blend the banana chunks, milk, cocoa powder, peppermint extract, and honey (if using) in a blender.
3. Blend the ingredients until they are well combined and smooth.
4. Add some ice cubes and blend the smoothie until it is cold and foamy.
5. Pour the energizing chocolate mint protein smoothie into a glass, add fresh mint leaves as desired, and savor!

CHOCOLATE COCONUT BLISS SMOOTHIE

Ingredients:

- 1 ripe banana
- 1/2 cup coconut milk
- 1/2 cup Greek yogurt
- 2 tablespoons cocoa powder
- 1 tablespoon honey or sweetener of your choice (optional)
- 2 tablespoons shredded coconut
- Ice cubes (optional)

Instructions:

1. Cut the banana into chunks after peeling it.
2. Combine the banana chunks, Greek yogurt, cocoa powder, coconut milk, and honey (if using) in a blender.
3. Puree everything until it's creamy and smooth.
4. Add some ice cubes and blend the smoothie until it is cold and foamy.
5. Combine the coconut shavings.

6. Pour into a glass and, if preferred, top with additional coconut shreds. Enjoy the smoothie of tropical chocolate and coconut delight!

MAPLE WALNUT SMOOTHIE

Ingredients:

- 1 ripe banana
- 1/2 cup milk (dairy or plant-based)
- 2 tablespoons maple syrup
- 2 tablespoons walnut butter
- 1/4 teaspoon vanilla extract
- 1/4 teaspoon ground cinnamon
- Ice cubes (optional)
- Chopped walnuts for garnish (optional)

Instructions:

1. Cut the banana into chunks after peeling it.
2. Combine the chunks of banana, milk, maple syrup, walnut butter, vanilla essence, and ground cinnamon in a blender.
3. Blend the ingredients until they are well combined and smooth.
4. Add some ice cubes and blend the smoothie until it is cold and foamy.
5. Pour the delicious maple walnut smoothie into a glass, top with chopped walnuts, and savor!

PISTACHIO CHOCOLATE DREAM SMOOTHIE

Ingredients:

- 1 ripe banana
- 1 cup milk (dairy or plant-based)
- 1/4 cup shelled pistachios
- 2 tablespoons cocoa powder
- 1 tablespoon honey or sweetener of your choice (optional)
- Ice cubes (optional)

Instructions:

1. Cut the banana into chunks after peeling it.
2. Blend the banana pieces, milk, pistachios, cocoa powder, and honey (if using) together in a blender.
3. Puree everything until it's creamy and smooth.
4. Add some ice cubes and blend the smoothie until it is cold and foamy.
5. Pour the thick and nutty pistachio chocolate dream smoothie into a glass and savor!

CHOCOLATE AVOCADO MOUSSE SMOOTHIE

Ingredients:

- 1 ripe avocado
- 1 cup milk (dairy or plant-based)
- 2 tablespoons cocoa powder
- 2 tablespoons honey or sweetener of your choice
- 1/2 teaspoon vanilla extract
- Ice cubes (optional)

Instructions:

1. Halve the avocado, scoop out the flesh, and discard the pit.
2. Combine the avocado, milk, chocolate powder, honey, and vanilla extract in a blender.
3. Puree everything until it's creamy and smooth.
4. Add some ice cubes and blend the smoothie until it is cold and foamy.
5. Pour the velvety and decadent chocolate avocado mousse smoothie into a glass and enjoy!

CHOCOLATE ALMOND BUTTER BANANA SMOOTHIE

Ingredients:

- 1 ripe banana
- 2 tablespoons almond butter
- 1 cup milk (dairy or plant-based)
- 2 tablespoons cocoa powder
- 1 tablespoon honey or sweetener of your choice (optional)
- Ice cubes (optional)

Instructions:

1. Cut the banana into chunks after peeling it.
2. Combine the banana chunks, milk, cocoa powder, and honey (if using) in a blender.
3. Puree everything until it's creamy and smooth.
4. Add some ice cubes and blend the smoothie until it is cold and foamy.
5. Pour the delicious chocolate, almond butter, and banana concoction into a glass and savor it!

PEANUT BUTTER PRETZEL SMOOTHIE

Ingredients:

- 1 ripe banana
- 2 tablespoons peanut butter
- 1 cup milk (dairy or plant-based)
- 2 tablespoons cocoa powder
- 1 tablespoon honey or sweetener of your choice (optional)
- 1/4 cup pretzels
- Ice cubes (optional)

Instructions:

1. Cut the banana into chunks after peeling it.
2. Combine the banana chunks, milk, cocoa powder, and honey (if using) in a blender.
3. Puree everything until it's creamy and smooth.
4. Add some ice cubes and blend the smoothie until it is cold and foamy.
5. After adding the pretzels to the blender, pulse it slightly to crush them and mix them into the smoothie.
6. Pour into a glass; if preferred, top with a pretzel stick. Enjoy the smoothie with sweet and salty peanut butter and pretzels!

DOUBLE CHOCOLATE PROTEIN SHAKE

Ingredients:

- 1 ripe banana
- 1 cup milk (dairy or plant-based)

- 2 tablespoons chocolate protein powder
- 1 tablespoon cocoa powder
- 1 tablespoon honey or sweetener of your choice (optional)
- Ice cubes (optional)
- Chocolate shavings for garnish (optional)

Instructions:

1. Cut the banana into chunks after peeling it.
2. Blend the banana chunks, milk, cocoa powder, honey (if using), and chocolate protein powder in a blender.
3. Blend the ingredients until they are well combined and smooth.
4. Add some ice cubes and blend the smoothie until it is cold and foamy.
5. Pour into a glass and, if you like, top with chocolate shavings. Take pleasure in the decadent and protein-rich double chocolate protein shake.

CHOCOLATE COVERED ALMOND SMOOTHIE

Ingredients:

- 1 ripe banana
- 2 tablespoons almond butter
- 1 cup milk (dairy or plant-based)
- 2 tablespoons cocoa powder
- 1 tablespoon honey or sweetener of your choice (optional)
- 1/4 cup chocolate-covered almonds

- Ice cubes (optional)

Instructions:

1. Cut the banana into chunks after peeling it.
2. Combine the banana chunks, milk, cocoa powder, and honey (if using) in a blender.
3. Puree everything until it's creamy and smooth.
4. Add some ice cubes and blend the smoothie until it is cold and foamy.
5. Add the almonds wrapped in chocolate.
6. Pour into a glass and, if preferred, top with more chocolate-covered almonds. Enjoy the tasty almond smoothie with chocolate on top!

CHAPTER 8: SUPERFOOD BOOSTED SMOOTHIES

ACAI BERRY SUPERFOOD SMOOTHIE

Ingredients:

- 1 frozen acai packet or 2 tablespoons acai powder
- 1 ripe banana
- 1 cup mixed berries (such as blueberries, raspberries, and strawberries)
- 1 cup almond milk or coconut water
- 1 tablespoon honey or sweetener of your choice (optional)
- 1 tablespoon chia seeds (optional)
- Ice cubes (optional)

Instructions:

1. Blend the frozen acai packet with the banana, mixed berries, almond milk, coconut water, and any more honey you choose.
2. Purée everything until it's smooth and evenly distributed.
3. If preferred, add chia seeds and mix briefly one more.
4. Add a few ice cubes and blend the mixture until it is bubbly and chilled to make a more excellent smoothie.
5. Pour into a glass, and top with more chia seeds if preferred. Enjoy the superfood acai berry smoothie, which is high in antioxidants!

MATCHA GREEN TEA SUPERFOOD SMOOTHIE

Ingredients:

- 1 ripe banana
- 1 cup spinach or kale leaves
- 1 teaspoon matcha green tea powder
- 1 cup almond milk or coconut water
- 1 tablespoon honey or sweetener of your choice (optional)
- 1 tablespoon almond butter (optional)
- Ice cubes (optional)

Instructions:

1. Cut the banana into chunks after peeling it.
2. Blend the chunks of banana, spinach, or kale, matcha green tea powder, almond milk or coconut water, honey (if used), and almond butter (if using) in a blender.
3. Blend the ingredients until they are well combined and smooth.
4. Add some ice cubes and blend the smoothie until it is cold and foamy.
5. Pour the hydrating, nutrient-rich matcha green tea superfood smoothie into a glass and savor!

SPIRULINA BLUEBERRY BLAST

Ingredients:

- 1 cup frozen blueberries
- 1 ripe banana
- 1 tablespoon spirulina powder
- 1 cup almond milk or coconut water
- 1 tablespoon honey or sweetener of your choice (optional)
- 1 tablespoon flaxseed meal (optional)
- Ice cubes (optional)

Instructions:

1. Blend the frozen blueberries, banana, almond milk or coconut water, spirulina powder, honey (if used), and flaxseed meal (if used) in a blender.
2. Purée everything until it's smooth and evenly distributed.
3. Add some ice cubes and reblend the smoothie until it is cold and foamy.
4. Pour the nutrient-rich and colorful spirulina blueberry blast into a glass and savor!

TURMERIC GINGER IMMUNITY BOOSTER

Ingredients:

- 1 ripe banana
- 1 cup pineapple chunks
- 1 tablespoon fresh ginger, grated
- 1 teaspoon ground turmeric

- 1 cup coconut water or orange juice
- 1 tablespoon honey or sweetener of your choice (optional)
- Dash of black pepper (optional)
- Ice cubes (optional)

Instructions:

1. The banana should be peeled and chopped.
2. Banana and pineapple chunks, grated ginger, ground turmeric, coconut water or orange juice, honey (if using), and a pinch of black pepper (if using) should all be combined in a blender.
3. Everything should be thoroughly mixed and blended.
4. Add some ice cubes and blend once more when the smoothie is cold and foamy.
5. Place in a glass and sip.

GOJI BERRY POWER SMOOTHIE

Ingredients:

- 1 cup frozen mixed berries (such as strawberries, blueberries, and raspberries)
- 1 ripe banana
- 1 tablespoon goji berries
- 1 cup almond milk or coconut water
- 1 tablespoon honey or sweetener of your choice (optional)
- 1 tablespoon hemp seeds (optional)
- Ice cubes (optional)

Instructions:

1. Blend the frozen mixed berries, banana, goji berries, coconut water or almond milk, and honey (if using) in a blender.
2. Purée everything until it's smooth and evenly distributed.
3. If wanted, include hemp seeds and mix briefly once more.
4. Add a few ice cubes and blend the mixture until it is frothy and chilled to make a more excellent smoothie.
5. Pour the antioxidant-rich goji berry power smoothie into a glass and savor it!

CHIA SEED SUPERFOOD SMOOTHIE

Ingredients:
- 1 ripe banana
- 1 cup spinach or kale leaves
- 1 tablespoon chia seeds
- 1 cup coconut water or almond milk
- 1 tablespoon almond butter or peanut butter
- 1 tablespoon honey or sweetener of your choice (optional)
- Ice cubes (optional)

Instructions:
1. Cut the banana into chunks after peeling it.
2. Blend the banana chunks, spinach or kale leaves, chia seeds, almond milk or coconut water, almond butter or peanut butter, and any more honey you choose.
3. Blend the ingredients until they are well combined and smooth.
4. Add some ice cubes and blend the smoothie until it is cold and foamy.

5. Pour the nutrient-rich chia seed superfood smoothie into a glass and savor it!

KALE AND WHEATGRASS DETOX SMOOTHIE

Ingredients:

- 1 ripe banana
- 1 cup kale leaves
- 1 tablespoon wheatgrass powder
- 1 cup coconut water or green tea
- Juice of 1/2 lemon
- 1 tablespoon honey or sweetener of your choice (optional)
- Ice cubes (optional)

Instructions:

1. Cut the banana into chunks after peeling it.
2. In a blender, combine the pieces of banana, kale, wheatgrass powder, coconut water or green tea, lemon juice, and honey (if using).
3. Blend the ingredients until they are well combined and smooth.
4. Add some ice cubes and blend the smoothie until it is cold and foamy.
5. Pour the cleansing and revitalizing kale and wheatgrass smoothie into a glass and savor!

FLAXSEED AND BERRY ANTIOXIDANT SMOOTHIE

Ingredients:

- 1 cup mixed berries (such as strawberries, blueberries, and raspberries)
- 1 ripe banana
- 1 tablespoon ground flaxseeds
- 1 cup almond milk or coconut water
- 1 tablespoon honey or sweetener of your choice (optional)
- 1/4 teaspoon vanilla extract
- Ice cubes (optional)

Instructions:

1. In a blender, combine the mixed berries, banana, flaxseeds that have been ground, almond milk or coconut water, honey (if using), and vanilla extract.
2. Purée everything until it's smooth and evenly distributed.
3. Add some ice cubes and reblend the smoothie until it is cold and foamy.
4. Pour the flaxseed and berry smoothie into a glass and savor the antioxidant-rich treat!

MACA ENERGIZING SMOOTHIE

Ingredients:

- 1 ripe banana
- 1 cup almond milk or coconut water
- 1 tablespoon maca powder
- 1 tablespoon almond butter or peanut butter
- 1 tablespoon honey or sweetener of your choice (optional)
- Ice cubes (optional)

Instructions:

1. Cut the banana into chunks after peeling it.
2. In a blender, combine the banana chunks, maca powder, almond butter or peanut butter, and honey (if using).
3. Blend the ingredients until they are well combined and smooth.
4. Add some ice cubes and blend the smoothie until it is cold and foamy.
5. Pour the stimulating and nourishing maca smoothie into a glass and savor it!

HEMP SEED PROTEIN SMOOTHIE

Ingredients:

- 1 ripe banana
- 2 tablespoons hemp seeds
- 1 cup almond milk or coconut water
- 2 tablespoons cocoa powder

- 1 tablespoon honey or sweetener of your choice (optional)
- 1/2 teaspoon vanilla extract
- Ice cubes (optional)

Instructions:

1. Cut the banana into chunks after peeling it.
2. Combine the hemp seeds, banana chunks, almond milk or coconut water, chocolate powder, honey (if using), and vanilla extract in a blender.
3. Blend the ingredients until they are well combined and smooth.
4. Add some ice cubes and blend the smoothie until it is cold and foamy.
5. Pour the protein-rich hemp seed smoothie into a glass and savor it!

CACAO AND BANANA SUPERFOOD SMOOTHIE

Ingredients:

- 1 ripe banana
- 2 tablespoons cacao powder
- 1 cup almond milk or coconut water
- 1 tablespoon almond butter or peanut butter
- 1 tablespoon honey or sweetener of your choice (optional)
- Ice cubes (optional)

Instructions:

1. Cut the banana into chunks after peeling it.

2. In a blender, combine the banana chunks, cacao powder, almond milk, coconut water, peanut butter, and honey (if using).
3. Blend the ingredients until they are well combined and smooth.
4. Add some ice cubes and blend the smoothie until it is cold and foamy.
5. Pour the tasty and wholesome chocolate and banana superfood smoothie into a glass and savor it!

MORINGA GREEN POWER SMOOTHIE

Ingredients:

- 1 ripe banana
- 1 cup spinach or kale leaves
- 1 tablespoon moringa powder
- 1 cup coconut water or almond milk
- 1 tablespoon honey or sweetener of your choice (optional)
- Juice of 1/2 lemon
- Ice cubes (optional)

Instructions:

1. Cut the banana into chunks after peeling it.
2. In a blender, combine the chunks of banana, spinach, kale, moringa powder, coconut water or almond milk, honey (if used), and lemon juice.
3. Blend the ingredients until they are well combined and smooth.
4. Add some ice cubes and blend the smoothie until it is cold and foamy.

5. Pour the invigorating and nutrient-dense moringa green power smoothie into a glass and savor!

CAMU CAMU VITAMIN C BOOST SMOOTHIE

Ingredients:

- 1 cup frozen mixed berries (such as strawberries, blueberries, and raspberries)
- 1 ripe banana
- 1 tablespoon camu camu powder
- 1 cup orange juice
- 1 tablespoon honey or sweetener of your choice (optional)
- Ice cubes (optional)

Instructions:

1. Blend the orange juice, camu camu powder, frozen mixed berries, banana, and honey (if using) together in a blender.
2. Purée everything until it's smooth and evenly distributed.
3. Add some ice cubes and reblend the smoothie until it is cold and foamy.
4. Pour the vitamin-rich camu camu boost smoothie into a glass and savor it!

BEE POLLEN AND HONEY ENERGIZER

Ingredients:

- 1 ripe banana
- 1 cup almond milk or coconut water
- 2 tablespoons bee pollen
- 1 tablespoon honey or sweetener of your choice
- 1/4 teaspoon cinnamon
- Ice cubes (optional)

Instructions:

1. Slice the banana into chunks after peeling it.
2. Combine the cinnamon, bee pollen, almond milk or coconut water, and banana pieces in a blender.
3. Blend the ingredients thoroughly and smoothly.
4. Blend the smoothie again after adding some ice cubes to make it cold and foamy.
5. Pour the invigorating and nutrient-rich bee pollen and honey smoothie into a glass and savor!

COCONUT WATER-ELECTROLYTE SMOOTHIE

Ingredients:

- 1 ripe banana
- 1 cup coconut water
- 1/2 cup pineapple chunks
- 1/4 cup fresh orange juice
- 1 tablespoon chia seeds

- 1 tablespoon honey or sweetener of your choice (optional)
- Ice cubes (optional)

Instructions:

1. Cut the banana into chunks after peeling it.
2. Place the banana chunks, coconut water, pineapple chunks, orange juice, chia seeds, and honey (if using) in a blender and blend until smooth.
3. Blend the ingredients until they are well combined and smooth.
4. Add some ice cubes and blend the smoothie until it is cold and foamy.
5. Pour the smoothie of coconut water and electrolytes into a glass to drink.

QUINOA AND BLUEBERRY PROTEIN SMOOTHIE

Ingredients:

- 1/2 cup cooked quinoa
- 1 cup blueberries (fresh or frozen)
- 1 ripe banana
- 1 cup almond milk or Greek yogurt
- 2 tablespoons protein powder (vanilla or berry flavor)
- 1 tablespoon honey or sweetener of your choice (optional)
- Ice cubes (optional)

Instructions:

1. The cooked quinoa, blueberries, banana, almond milk or Greek yogurt, protein powder, and honey (if using) should all be combined in a blender.
2. Everything should be thoroughly mixed and blended.
3. Add some ice cubes and blend once more when the smoothie is cold and foamy.
4. Enjoy the protein-rich quinoa and blueberry smoothie by pouring it into a glass.

BAOBAB TROPICAL DELIGHT

Ingredients:
- 1 ripe mango, peeled and pitted
- 1 ripe banana
- 1 tablespoon baobab powder
- 1 cup coconut water or pineapple juice
- 1 tablespoon honey or sweetener of your choice (optional)
- Ice cubes (optional)

Instructions:
1. Mango, banana, baobab powder, coconut water or pineapple juice, and honey (if using) should all be combined in a blender.
2. Purée everything until it's smooth and evenly distributed.
3. Add some ice cubes and reblend the smoothie until it is cold and foamy.
4. Pour into a glass and savor the baobab smoothie's tropical deliciousness!

CHLORELLA CLEANSING GREEN SMOOTHIE

Ingredients:

- 1 ripe banana
- 1 cup spinach or kale leaves
- 1 tablespoon chlorella powder
- 1/2 cucumber, peeled and chopped
- Juice of 1/2 lemon
- 1 cup coconut water or almond milk
- 1 tablespoon honey or sweetener of your choice (optional)
- Ice cubes (optional)

Instructions:

1. Cut the banana into chunks after peeling it.
2. Blend the chunks of banana, spinach or kale, chlorella powder, cucumber, lemon juice, coconut water, almond milk, and honey (if using) together in a blender.
3. Blend the ingredients until they are well combined and smooth.
4. Add some ice cubes and blend the smoothie until it is cold and foamy.
5. Pour into a glass and savor the chlorella green smoothie's purifying and detoxifying properties!

MAQUI BERRY ANTIOXIDANT BURST

Ingredients:

- 1 cup frozen mixed berries (such as blueberries, raspberries, and strawberries)
- 1 ripe banana
- 1 tablespoon maqui berry powder
- 1 cup almond milk or coconut water
- 1 tablespoon honey or sweetener of your choice (optional)
- Ice cubes (optional)

Instructions:

1. Blend the frozen mixed berries, banana, maqui berry powder, almond milk, coconut water, and any additional honey you like.
2. Purée everything until it's smooth and evenly distributed.
3. Add some ice cubes and reblend the smoothie until it is cold and foamy.
4. Pour into a glass and savor the flavorful, antioxidant-rich maqui berry smoothie!

HEMP HEART AND MANGO SMOOTHIE

Ingredients:

- 1 ripe mango, peeled and pitted
- 1 ripe banana
- 2 tablespoons hemp hearts
- 1 cup almond milk or coconut water

- 1 tablespoon honey or sweetener of your choice (optional)
- Ice cubes (optional)

Instructions:

1. Place the mango, banana, hemp hearts, almond milk, coconut water, and more honey in a blender.
2. Purée everything until it's smooth and evenly distributed.
3. Add some ice cubes and reblend the smoothie until it is cold and foamy.
4. Pour the creamy, wholesome hemp heart and mango smoothie into a glass and savor it!

CHAPTER 9: DETOX AND CLEANSING ELIXIR BLENDS

GREEN DETOX ELIXIR

Ingredients:

- 1 cup spinach
- 1 cucumber
- 2 celery stalks
- 1 green apple
- Juice of 1 lemon
- 1-inch piece of ginger
- 1 cup coconut water

Instructions:

1. Thoroughly wash each component.
2. Finely chop the cucumber, celery stalks, and green apple.
3. Grate and peel the ginger.
4. Combine all the ingredients in a blender.
5. Blend until thoroughly integrated and smooth.
6. To get rid of any pulp, sieve the mixture if required.
7. Serve cold and take pleasure in it!

BEET AND GINGER CLEANSING TONIC

Ingredients:

- 1 medium beet
- 1-inch piece of ginger
- Juice of 1 lemon
- 1 tablespoon honey
- 2 cups water

Instructions:

1. Peel the beet and slice it into small pieces.
2. Ginger should be peeled and grated.
3. Combine the beet, ginger, lemon juice, honey, and water in a blender.
4. Blend until thoroughly integrated and smooth.
5. To get rid of the pulp, strain the mixture.
6. Distribute chilled, and savor!

CUCUMBER AND MINT DETOX WATER

Ingredients:

- 1 cucumber
- 10-12 fresh mint leaves
- 2 cups water
- Ice cubes (optional)

Instructions:

1. Clean the mint and cucumber leaves.
2. Cut the cucumber into rounds with refined edges.
3. Place the cucumber slices and mint leaves in a pitcher.
4. Fill the pitcher with water.
5. If desired, add ice cubes.
6. After thoroughly stirring, place the mixture in the refrigerator for a few hours to let the flavors meld.
7. Serve cold and take pleasure in it!

LEMON TURMERIC DETOX ELIXIR

Ingredients:

- Juice of 2 lemons
- 1 teaspoon turmeric powder
- 1 tablespoon honey
- Pinch of black pepper
- 2 cups warm water

Instructions:

1. Mix the lemon juice, turmeric powder, honey, and black pepper to make a glass.

2. Continue to stir until all of the ingredients are thoroughly combined.
3. Fill the glass with warm water, then stir once more.
4. You may either serve it hot or cool it and do it with ice.
5. Enjoy!

DANDELION AND BERRY DETOX SMOOTHIE

Ingredients:
- 1 cup dandelion greens
- 1 cup mixed berries (such as strawberries, blueberries, and raspberries)
- 1 banana
- 1 cup almond milk
- 1 tablespoon chia seeds

Instructions:
1. Clean the dandelion berries and greens.
2. Put the banana, almond milk, chia seeds, mixed berries, dandelion greens, and chia seeds in a blender.
3. Blend until creamy and smooth.
4. Enjoy when serving chilled!

APPLE CIDER VINEGAR MORNING BOOST

Ingredients:

- 2 tablespoons apple cider vinegar
- 1 tablespoon honey
- Juice of 1 lemon
- 1 cup warm water

Instructions:

1. Combine the lemon juice, honey, and apple cider vinegar in a glass.
2. Fill the glass with warm water and thoroughly swirl to combine the ingredients.
3. Take it on an empty stomach first thing in the morning.
4. Relish the revitalizing boost!

CHARCOAL LEMONADE DETOX ELIXIR

Ingredients:

- 2 capsules of activated charcoal
- Juice of 4 lemons
- 4 cups water
- 1 tablespoon maple syrup or honey (optional)
- Ice cubes (optional)

Instructions:

1. Remove the powder from the activated charcoal capsules and pour it into a pitcher.
2. Squeeze the lemons and pour the juice into the pitcher.
3. Fill the pitcher with water and thoroughly mix it in.

4. You can add honey or maple syrup for a hint of sweetness if you'd like.
5. If desired, add ice cubes.
6. Distribute chilled, and savor!

PARSLEY AND LEMON CLEANSING ELIXIR

Ingredients:

- 1 bunch of fresh parsley
- Juice of 2 lemons
- 4 cups water
- 1 tablespoon honey (optional)
- Ice cubes (optional)

Instructions:

1. Thoroughly wash the parsley and cut off any tough stalks.
2. Blend the parsley, lemon juice, water, and honey (if using) in a blender.
3. Blend until thoroughly integrated and smooth.
4. To get rid of any pulp, sieve the mixture if required.
5. If desired, add ice cubes.
6. Enjoy the purifying elixir after serving chilled!

WATERMELON AND CUCUMBER DETOX WATER

Ingredients:

- 2 cups cubed watermelon
- 1 cucumber, sliced
- 10-12 fresh mint leaves
- 2 cups water
- Ice cubes (optional)

Instructions:

1. Mix the cubed watermelon, cucumber slices, and fresh mint in a pitcher.
2. Fill the pitcher with water.
3. If desired, add ice cubes.
4. After thoroughly stirring, place the mixture in the refrigerator for a few hours to let the flavors meld.
5. Serve the detox water-cooled, and savor the cooling effects!

GINGER LEMON CLEANSING SMOOTHIE

Ingredients:

- 1 cup chopped kale
- 1 ripe banana
- 1-inch piece of ginger
- Juice of 1 lemon
- 1 cup coconut water
- 1 tablespoon flaxseeds (optional)

Instructions:

1. Thoroughly wash the kale and cut off the tough stems.
2. Combine the kale, ginger, banana, coconut water, lemon juice, and flaxseeds (if using).
3. Blend until creamy and smooth.
4. Serve the cooled smoothie, and savor it!

PAPAYA AND LIME DIGESTIVE ELIXIR

Ingredients:

- 1 cup ripe papaya, diced
- Juice of 1 lime
- 1 tablespoon honey
- 2 cups water

Instructions:

1. Combine the ripe papaya, lime juice, honey, and water in a blender.
2. Blend until thoroughly integrated and smooth.
3. To get rid of any pulp, sift the mixture if required.
4. Enjoy the elixir of digestion after serving chilled!

CRANBERRY DETOX ELIXIR

Ingredients:

- 1 cup cranberries
- Juice of 1 lemon
- 1 tablespoon maple syrup
- 2 cups water

Instructions:

1. Combine the cranberries, water, maple syrup, and lemon juice in a blender.
2. Blend until thoroughly integrated and smooth.
3. To get rid of any pulp, sift the mixture if required.
4. Serve the detox elixir cold, and enjoy!

CARROT AND ORANGE CLEANSING ELIXIR

Ingredients:

- 2 large carrots
- Juice of 2 oranges
- 1-inch piece of ginger
- 1 tablespoon honey
- 2 cups water

Instructions:

1. Peel the carrots and cut them into small pieces.
2. To obtain the oranges' fresh juice, juice them.
3. Grate and peel the ginger.
4. In a blender, combine the grated ginger, orange juice, water, honey, and carrots that have been diced.
5. Blend until thoroughly integrated and smooth.
6. To get rid of any pulp, sieve the mixture if required.
7. Enjoy the purifying elixir after serving cooled!

BLUEBERRY AND ALOE VERA DETOX SMOOTHIE

Ingredients:

- 1 cup blueberries
- 1 cup almond milk
- 1 tablespoon aloe vera gel
- 1 tablespoon honey
- 1 tablespoon chia seeds

Instructions:

1. Wash the blueberries first.
2. Combine the blueberries, almond milk, honey, aloe vera gel, and chia seeds in a blender.
3. Blend until creamy and smooth.
4. Enjoy the detox smoothie after serving it chilled!

PINEAPPLE MINT DETOX WATER

Ingredients:

- 1 cup pineapple chunks
- 10-12 fresh mint leaves
- 2 cups water
- Ice cubes (optional)

Instructions:

1. Combine the pineapple chunks and fresh mint leaves in a pitcher.
2. Fill the pitcher with water.

3. If desired, add ice cubes.
4. After thoroughly stirring, place the mixture in the refrigerator for a few hours to let the flavors meld.
5. Serve the detox water-cooled, and savor the cooling effects!

KALE AND LEMON CLEANSING ELIXIR

Ingredients:

- 2 cups kale leaves
- Juice of 2 lemons
- 1 cucumber
- 1 green apple
- 1-inch piece of ginger
- 2 cups water

Instructions:

1. Wash the cucumber, green apple, and kale leaves.
2. Cut the kale's rough stems off.
3. Roughly chop the cucumber and green apple.
4. Grate and peel the ginger.
5. Combine the kale leaves, lemon juice, cucumber, green apple, grated ginger, and water in a blender.
6. Blend until thoroughly integrated and smooth.
7. To get rid of any pulp, sieve the mixture if required.
8. Enjoy the purifying elixir after serving chilled!

GRAPEFRUIT AND ROSEMARY DETOX ELIXIR

Ingredients:

- 2 grapefruits
- 2 sprigs of fresh rosemary
- 1 tablespoon honey
- 2 cups water

Instructions:

1. Extract the fresh juice from the grapefruits.
2. In a saucepan, gently boil the grapefruit juice and rosemary sprigs.
3. To allow the flavors to meld, let it cook for about 5 minutes.
4. Take the rosemary sprigs out of the pot.
5. Add the honey and whisk to combine.
6. Permit the mixture to cool.
7. Stir well after adding water to the chilled grapefruit mixture.
8. Serve cooled, then take a sip of the revitalizing detox beverage.

BEETROOT AND CARROT DETOX JUICE

Ingredients:

- 2 beetroots
- 3 carrots
- 1-inch piece of ginger
- Juice of 1 lemon
- 2 cups water

Instructions:

1. Wash the ginger, carrots, and beets.
2. Peel the carrots and beets, then cut them into small pieces.
3. Grate and peel the ginger.
4. Combine the water, grated ginger, diced carrots, beets, and lemon juice in a blender.
5. Blend until thoroughly integrated and smooth.
6. To get rid of any pulp, sieve the mixture if required.
7. Serve the detox juice cooled, and savor it!

MINT AND LIME REFRESHING DETOX ELIXIR

Ingredients:

- 10-12 fresh mint leaves
- Juice of 2 limes
- 1 tablespoon honey
- 2 cups water
- Ice cubes (optional)

Instructions:

1. Clean the mint leaves first.
2. Mix the mint leaves' flavors in a pitcher to bring out the flavors.
3. Squeeze the limes and pour the juice into the pitcher.
4. Fill the pitcher with honey and water, then thoroughly mix the ingredients.
5. If desired, add ice cubes.
6. To enable the flavors to meld, let it sit in the fridge for a few hours.
7. Serve cooled, then take a sip of the revitalizing detox beverage.

SPINACH AND PINEAPPLE CLEANSING SMOOTHIE

Ingredients:

- 2 cups fresh spinach leaves
- 1 cup pineapple chunks
- 1 banana
- 1 cup coconut water
- 1 tablespoon flaxseeds (optional)

Instructions:

1. Clean the spinach leaves first.
2. Place the spinach leaves, pineapple chunks, banana, coconut water, and flaxseeds (if using) in a blender and puree until smooth.
3. Blend until creamy and smooth.
4. Serve the cooled smoothie, and savor it!

CITRUS IMMUNITY BLAST

Ingredients:

- 1 orange, peeled
- 1 grapefruit, peeled
- 1 lemon, peeled
- 1 cup pineapple chunks
- 1 cup coconut water
- 1 tablespoon honey (optional)

Instructions:

1. Fill a blender with all the ingredients.
2. Blend until creamy and smooth.
3. Taste, and if desired, add honey.
4. Pour into a glass, then take a sip.

BERRY ANTIOXIDANT IMMUNITY SMOOTHIE

Ingredients:

- 1 cup mixed berries (strawberries, blueberries, raspberries)
- 1 cup spinach leaves
- 1 banana
- 1 cup almond milk (or any milk of your choice)
- 1 tablespoon chia seeds

Instructions:

1. Fill a blender with all the ingredients.
2. Blend until creamy and smooth.
3. Pour the mixture into a glass to serve.

GINGER TURMERIC IMMUNE BOOSTER

Ingredients:

- 1-inch piece of ginger, peeled and grated
- 1 teaspoon turmeric powder
- 1 cup coconut water
- 1 tablespoon honey (optional)
- Juice of 1 lemon

Instructions:

1. Fill a blender with coconut water, grated ginger, turmeric powder, honey (if using), and lemon juice.
2. Blend until smooth and well-combined.

3. Pour into a glass, then take a sip.

PINEAPPLE ORANGE VITAMIN C SMOOTHIE

Ingredients:

- 1 cup pineapple chunks
- 1 orange, peeled
- 1 cup Greek yogurt
- 1 tablespoon honey (optional)
- Ice cubes (optional)

Instructions:

1. Combine the pineapple chunks, orange peel, Greek yogurt, honey (if using), and optional ice cubes in a blender.
2. Blend until creamy and smooth.
3. Pour into a cold glass and serve.

SPINACH KIWI IMMUNITY ELIXIR

Ingredients:

- 1 cup spinach leaves
- 2 kiwis, peeled and sliced
- 1 banana
- 1 cup coconut water
- 1 tablespoon honey (optional)

Instructions:

1. Fill a blender with spinach leaves, kiwis, bananas, coconut water, and honey (if preferred).
2. Blend until creamy and smooth.
3. Pour into a glass, then take a sip.

MANGO GINGER IMMUNE SUPPORT SMOOTHIE

Ingredients:

- 1 cup mango chunks
- 1-inch piece of ginger peeled
- 1 cup orange juice
- 1/2 cup Greek yogurt
- 1 tablespoon flaxseeds (optional)

Instructions:

1. In a blender, combine the mango chunks, ginger that has been peeled, orange juice, Greek yogurt, and flaxseeds (if using).
2. Blend until creamy and smooth.
3. Pour the mixture into a glass to serve.

ELDERBERRY IMMUNE DEFENSE BLEND

Ingredients:

- 1 cup elderberries
- 1 cup blueberries
- 1 cup almond milk (or any milk of your choice)
- 1 tablespoon honey (optional)

- 1 teaspoon cinnamon

Instructions:

1. Fill a blender with elderberries, blueberries, almond milk, honey (if using), and cinnamon.
2. Blend until smooth and well-combined.
3. Pour into a glass, then take a sip.

BLUEBERRY POMEGRANATE IMMUNITY POWERHOUSE

Ingredients:

- 1 cup blueberries
- 1/2 cup pomegranate juice
- 1 cup spinach leaves
- 1 banana
- 1 cup coconut water

Instructions:

1. Combine the blueberries, pomegranate juice, spinach, banana, and coconut water in a blender.
2. Blend until creamy and smooth.
3. Pour the mixture into a glass to serve.

CARROT GINGER IMMUNE BOOST SMOOTHIE

Ingredients:

- 1 large carrot, peeled and chopped

- 1-inch piece of ginger peeled
- 1 orange, peeled
- 1 cup coconut water
- 1 tablespoon honey (optional)

Instructions:

1. Fill a blender with coconut water, diced carrot, ginger, citrus, and honey (if desired).
2. Blend until smooth and well-combined.
3. Pour into a glass, then take a sip.

GREEN TEA CITRUS IMMUNE ELIXIR

Ingredients:

- 1 green tea bag
- 1 cup boiling water
- 1 orange, peeled
- 1 lemon, peeled
- 1 tablespoon honey (optional)
- Ice cubes (optional)

Instructions:

1. Let the green tea bag steep for a few minutes in boiling water. Take out the tea bag, then let the tea cool.
2. In a blender, combine the iced green tea, peeled orange, lemon, and honey (if using).
3. Blend until thoroughly integrated and smooth.
4. If desired, mix again after adding ice cubes.
5. Transfer to a glass and serve.

BEETROOT BERRY ANTIOXIDANT SMOOTHIE

Ingredients:

- 1 small beetroot, peeled and chopped
- 1 cup mixed berries (strawberries, blueberries, raspberries)
- 1 banana
- 1 cup almond milk (or any milk of your choice)
- 1 tablespoon honey (optional)

Instructions:

1. Fill a blender with the diced beets, mixed berries, banana, almond milk, and optional honey.
2. Blend until creamy and smooth.
3. Pour the mixture into a glass to serve.

CRANBERRY IMMUNE RECOVERY SMOOTHIE

Ingredients:

- 1 cup cranberries (fresh or frozen)
- 1 orange, peeled
- 1/2 cup Greek yogurt
- 1 tablespoon chia seeds
- 1 tablespoon honey (optional)

Instructions:

1. In a blender, combine the cranberries, orange peel, Greek yogurt, chia seeds, and honey (if using).
2. Blend until smooth and well-combined.
3. Pour into a glass, then take a sip.

PUMPKIN SPICE IMMUNITY SMOOTHIE

Ingredients:

- 1 cup pumpkin puree
- 1 ripe banana
- 1 cup almond milk (or any milk of your choice)
- 1 tablespoon honey (optional)
- 1/2 teaspoon pumpkin spice mix

Instructions:

1. In a blender, combine the ripe pumpkin puree, banana, almond milk, honey (if desired), and pumpkin spice blend.
2. Blend until creamy and smooth.
3. Pour the mixture into a glass to serve.

KIWI LIME VITAMIN C BLAST

Ingredients:

- 2 kiwis, peeled and sliced
- Juice of 2 limes
- 1 cup spinach leaves
- 1 cup coconut water
- 1 tablespoon honey (optional)

Instructions:

1. Fill a blender with the kiwis, lime juice, spinach leaves, coconut water, and honey (if using).
2. Blend until thoroughly integrated and smooth.
3. Pour into a glass, then take a sip.

SPINACH MUSHROOM IMMUNITY ELIXIR

Ingredients:

- 1 cup spinach leaves
- 1 cup mushrooms, sliced
- 1 banana
- 1 cup almond milk (or any milk of your choice)
- 1 tablespoon almond butter (or any nut butter of your choice)

Instructions:

1. Combine the spinach leaves, sliced mushrooms, banana, almond milk, and almond butter in a blender.
2. Blend until creamy and smooth.
3. Pour the mixture into a glass to serve.

CHERRY LIME ANTIOXIDANT SMOOTHIE

Ingredients:

- 1 cup cherries (fresh or frozen)
- Juice of 2 limes
- 1 cup Greek yogurt
- 1 tablespoon honey (optional)

- Ice cubes (optional)

Instructions:

1. Fill a blender with cherries, lime juice, Greek yogurt, honey, and optional ice cubes.
2. Blend until thoroughly integrated and smooth.
3. Pour into a cold glass and serve.

ORANGE TURMERIC GINGER IMMUNE ELIXIR

Ingredients:

- Juice of 2 oranges
- 1 teaspoon turmeric powder
- 1-inch piece of ginger peeled
- 1 tablespoon honey (optional)
- 1 cup coconut water

Instructions:

1. Combine orange juice, coconut water, turmeric powder, peeled ginger, and honey in a blender.
2. Blend until thoroughly integrated and smooth.
3. Pour into a glass, then take a sip.

PAPAYA MINT IMMUNITY REFRESHER

Ingredients:

- 1 cup papaya chunks
- Juice of 1 lemon

- Handful of fresh mint leaves
- 1 cup coconut water
- 1 tablespoon honey (optional)
- Ice cubes (optional)

Instructions:

1. Fill a blender with the chunks of papaya, lemon juice, mint leaves, coconut water, honey, and ice cubes, if preferred.
2. Blend until thoroughly integrated and smooth.
3. Pour into a cold glass and serve.

RASPBERRY LEMON IMMUNE SUPPORT SMOOTHIE

Ingredients:

- 1 cup raspberries
- Juice of 2 lemons
- 1 banana
- 1 cup almond milk (or any milk of your choice)
- 1 tablespoon honey (optional)

Instructions:

1. In a blender, combine raspberries, lemon juice, banana, almond milk, and honey (if using).
2. Blend until creamy and smooth.
3. Pour into a glass, then take a sip.

WATERMELON BASIL HYDRATION AND IMMUNITY BLEND

Ingredients:

- 2 cups diced watermelon
- Juice of 1 lime
- Handful of fresh basil leaves
- 1 tablespoon honey (optional)
- Ice cubes (optional)

Instructions:

1. In a blender, combine the diced watermelon, lime juice, fresh basil leaves, honey (if used), and ice cubes (if used).
2. Blend until thoroughly integrated and smooth.
3. Pour into a cold glass and serve.

PRE-WORKOUT POWER BOOSTER

Ingredients:

- 1 cup unsweetened almond milk
- 1 ripe banana
- 1 scoop of your preferred pre-workout powder
- 1 tablespoon almond butter
- 1 tablespoon honey
- 1/2 teaspoon cinnamon
- Ice cubes (optional)

Instructions:

1. Fill a blender with all the ingredients.
2. Blend until creamy and smooth.
3. If preferred, add ice cubes and blend once more for a colder texture.
4. Pour into a glass and take a sip before going out.

GREEN ENERGY BURST SMOOTHIE

Ingredients:

- 1 cup spinach
- 1/2 cup kale
- 1 ripe banana
- 1/2 cup green grapes

- 1/2 cup pineapple chunks
- 1 tablespoon chia seeds
- 1 cup coconut water

Instructions:

1. Fill a blender with all the ingredients.
2. Blend until thoroughly integrated and smooth.
3. If the mixture is too thick, thin it with additional or coconut water.
4. Pour into a glass and savor the revitalizing rush of green energy.

BANANA NUT ENERGIZER

Ingredients:

- 1 ripe banana
- 1 cup almond milk
- 2 tablespoons almond butter
- 1 tablespoon honey
- 1/4 cup rolled oats
- 1/4 teaspoon vanilla extract
- Pinch of salt
- Ice cubes (optional)

Instructions:

1. Combine all the ingredients in a blender.
2. Blend until creamy and smooth.
3. Blend the smoothie again after adding some ice cubes if you prefer more relaxed.
4. Pour the banana nut energizer into a glass and enjoy.

TROPICAL ELECTROLYTE REFUEL

- Ingredients:
- 1 cup coconut water
- 1/2 cup pineapple chunks
- 1/2 cup mango chunks
- 1 ripe banana
- 1/4 cup orange juice
- 1 tablespoon lime juice
- 1 tablespoon honey
- Ice cubes (optional)

Instructions:

1. Fill a blender with all the ingredients.
2. Blend until thoroughly integrated and smooth.
3. For a cool, refreshing drink, ice cubes may be added and blended again.
4. Pour the tropical electrolyte refuel into a glass and sip.

CHOCOLATE ESPRESSO PROTEIN SHAKE

Ingredients:

- 1 cup unsweetened almond milk
- 1 scoop of chocolate protein powder
- 1 shot of espresso or 1/2 cup of strong brewed coffee, cooled
- 1 tablespoon almond butter
- 1 tablespoon cocoa powder
- 1/2 teaspoon vanilla extract

- Ice cubes (optional)

Instructions:

1. Combine all the ingredients in a blender.
2. Blend until it's creamy and smooth.
3. Add some ice cubes and combine one more for a cooler shake.
4. Pour the chocolate espresso protein shake into a glass and enjoy.

BERRY BLAST ENDURANCE SMOOTHIE

Ingredients:

- 1 cup mixed berries (strawberries, blueberries, raspberries)
- 1/2 cup Greek yogurt
- 1/2 cup almond milk
- 1 tablespoon honey
- 1 tablespoon flax seeds
- 1/2 teaspoon vanilla extract
- Ice cubes (optional)

Instructions:

1. Fill a blender with all the ingredients.
2. Blend until thoroughly integrated and smooth.
3. Add ice cubes and blend once more for a smooth, refreshing texture if preferred.
4. Pour the berry blast endurance smoothie into a glass and sip.

MATCHA GREEN TEA ENERGY ELIXIR

Ingredients:

- 1 teaspoon matcha green tea powder
- 1 cup almond milk
- 1/2 banana
- 1 tablespoon honey
- 1/4 teaspoon vanilla extract
- Ice cubes (optional)

Instructions:

1. Blend a banana, almond milk, matcha green tea powder, honey, and vanilla essence in a blender.
2. Blend until creamy and smooth.
3. If preferred, add ice cubes and blend again for a cold elixir.
4. Pour the matcha green tea energy drink into a glass and enjoy.

BLUEBERRY ALMOND RECOVERY SHAKE

Ingredients:

- 1 cup almond milk
- 1/2 cup blueberries
- 1/4 cup almond butter
- 1 tablespoon honey
- 1/2 teaspoon cinnamon
- 1/2 cup plain Greek yogurt
- Ice cubes (optional)

Instructions:

1. Blend the items in a blender.
2. Blend everything thoroughly until it's smooth.
3. For a fantastic shake, add ice cubes and combine once more.
4. Enjoy the blueberry almond recovery smoothie after pouring it into a glass.

PINEAPPLE COCONUT HYDRATING SMOOTHIE

Ingredients:

- 1 cup coconut water
- 1/2 cup pineapple chunks
- 1/2 cup cucumber, peeled and chopped
- 1/4 cup fresh mint leaves
- Juice of 1 lime
- 1 tablespoon honey
- Ice cubes (optional)

Instructions:

1. Combine lime juice, coconut water, pineapple pieces, cucumber, mint leaves, and honey in a blender.
2. Blend until thoroughly integrated and smooth.
3. Add ice cubes and blend again for a simple, hydrating smoothie if preferred.
4. Pour the pineapple coconut hydrating smoothie into a glass and sip.

PEANUT BUTTER BANANA POWER SMOOTHIE

Ingredients:

- 1 ripe banana
- 1 cup almond milk
- 2 tablespoons peanut butter
- 1 tablespoon honey
- 1/4 cup oats
- 1/2 teaspoon cinnamon
- Ice cubes (optional)

Instructions:

1. Fill a blender with all the ingredients.
2. Blend until creamy and smooth.
3. Blend the smoothie again after adding some ice cubes if you prefer more relaxed.
4. Pour the peanut butter banana power smoothie into a glass and enjoy.

CITRUS BEET PRE-WORKOUT BLEND

Ingredients:

- 1 small beet, peeled and chopped
- 1 orange, peeled and segmented
- 1/2 grapefruit, peeled and segmented
- 1/2 lemon, juiced
- 1 tablespoon honey
- 1 cup coconut water

- Ice cubes (optional)

Instructions:
1. Fill a blender with all the ingredients.
2. Blend until thoroughly integrated and smooth.
3. Add ice cubes and blend again to create a cold pre-workout blend if preferred.
4. Pour the citrus beet pre-workout mixture into a glass and savor.

CHOCOLATE CHERRY WORKOUT FUEL

Ingredients:
- 1 cup almond milk
- 1 cup frozen cherries
- 1 scoop of chocolate protein powder
- 1 tablespoon almond butter
- 1 tablespoon cacao powder
- 1 tablespoon honey
- Ice cubes (optional)

Instructions:
1. Combine almond milk, cacao powder, honey, almond butter, frozen cherries, and chocolate protein powder in a blender.
2. Blend until creamy and smooth.
3. Blend the smoothie again after adding some ice cubes if you prefer more relaxed.
4. Pour the chocolate cherry exercise fuel into a glass and sip.

SPINACH AVOCADO ENERGY ELIXIR

Ingredients:

- 1 cup spinach
- 1/2 ripe avocado
- 1 ripe banana
- 1 cup coconut water
- 1 tablespoon chia seeds
- 1 tablespoon honey
- Juice of 1 lime
- Ice cubes (optional)

Instructions:

1. Fill a blender with all the ingredients.
2. Blend until thoroughly integrated and smooth.
3. To make a refreshing elixir, add ice cubes and blend again if desired.
4. Pour the spinach avocado energy drink into a glass and enjoy.

MANGO TURMERIC ENERGIZING SMOOTHIE

Ingredients:

- 1 cup frozen mango chunks
- 1/2 cup plain Greek yogurt
- 1 cup almond milk
- 1 tablespoon honey
- 1/2 teaspoon turmeric powder

- 1/2 teaspoon ginger powder
- Ice cubes (optional)

Instructions:

1. Combine Greek yogurt, almond milk, honey, turmeric powder, and ginger powder with chunks of frozen mango in a blender.
2. Blend until creamy and smooth.
3. Blend the smoothie again after adding some ice cubes if you prefer more relaxed.
4. Pour into a glass and savor the energetic mango turmeric smoothie.

CHIA SEED PUDDING ENERGY BOOSTER

Ingredients:

- 2 tablespoons chia seeds
- 1 cup almond milk
- 1 tablespoon honey or maple syrup
- 1/2 teaspoon vanilla extract
- Fresh fruits and nuts for topping (optional)

Instructions:

1. Combine the chia seeds, almond milk, honey or maple syrup, and vanilla extract in a container or bowl.
2. To thoroughly combine all the ingredients, stir well.
3. Allow the mixture to rest for approximately 10 minutes, stirring occasionally to avoid clumping.
4. Could you give it one last stir once the chia seeds have soaked up the liquid and reached a pudding-like consistency?

5. If preferred, add fresh fruits and nuts to the top for taste and additional energy.
6. Snack on the chia seed pudding to improve your stamina.

RASPBERRY LEMONADE ELECTROLYTE SMOOTHIE

Ingredients:
- 1 cup raspberries
- Juice of 2 lemons
- 1 cup coconut water
- 1 tablespoon honey
- Pinch of salt
- Ice cubes (optional)

Instructions:
1. Fill a blender with all the ingredients.
2. Blend until thoroughly integrated and smooth.
3. For a cooled smoothie, if preferred, add ice cubes and blend again.
4. Pour the hydrating raspberry lemonade electrolyte smoothie into a glass and savor it.

WATERMELON MINT HYDRATING REFRESHER

Ingredients:

- 2 cups cubed watermelon
- Juice of 1 lime
- Few fresh mint leaves
- 1 cup coconut water
- Ice cubes (optional)

Instructions:

1. Combine coconut water, lime juice, mint leaves, and watermelon in a blender.
2. Blend until thoroughly integrated and smooth.
3. If preferred, add ice cubes and blend again for a hydrating and refreshing refresher.
4. Pour the watermelon mint hydrating refresher into a glass and sip.

PUMPKIN SPICE PROTEIN ENERGY SHAKE

Ingredients:

- 1 cup almond milk
- 1/2 cup canned pumpkin puree
- 1 scoop vanilla protein powder
- 1 tablespoon almond butter
- 1 tablespoon maple syrup
- 1/2 teaspoon pumpkin spice
- Ice cubes (optional)

Instructions:

1. In a blender, combine the following ingredients: almond milk, pumpkin puree, vanilla protein powder, almond butter, maple syrup, and pumpkin spice.
2. Blend until creamy and smooth.
3. Add some ice cubes and combine one more for a cooler shake.
4. Pour the pumpkin spice protein energy smoothie into a glass, then sip.

KIWI LIME ELECTROLYTE POWERHOUSE

Ingredients:

- 2 kiwis, peeled and sliced
- Juice of 2 limes
- 1 cup coconut water
- 1 tablespoon honey
- Pinch of salt
- Ice cubes (optional)

Instructions:

1. Combine the kiwis, lime juice, coconut water, honey, and salt in a blender.
2. Blend until thoroughly integrated and smooth.
3. Add ice cubes and mix one more for a cooled and revitalizing powerful smoothie if preferred.
4. Pour into a glass and enjoy the electrolyte powerhouse that is kiwi lime.

ACAI BERRY STAMINA SMOOTHIE

Ingredients:

- 1 pack of frozen acai berry puree
- 1 ripe banana
- 1 cup almond milk
- 1 tablespoon almond butter
- 1 tablespoon honey
- Ice cubes (optional)

Instructions:

1. Combine the acai berry puree, honey, ripe banana, almond milk, and almond butter in a blender.
2. Blend until creamy and smooth.
3. Blend the smoothie again after adding some ice cubes if you prefer more relaxed.
4. Pour the acai berry stamina smoothie into a glass and sip.

GREEN DETOX AND SLIMMING SMOOTHIE

Ingredients:

- 1 cup spinach
- 1 green apple, cored and chopped
- 1/2 cucumber, chopped
- 1/2 lemon, juiced
- 1/2 cup unsweetened almond milk
- 1 tablespoon chia seeds
- Ice cubes (optional)

Instructions:

1. Fill a blender with all the ingredients.
2. Blend until creamy and smooth.
3. For a cooled smoothie, if preferred, add ice cubes and blend again.
4. Pour into a glass, then take a sip.

BLUEBERRY PROTEIN SLIMMING SHAKE

Ingredients:

- 1 cup frozen blueberries
- 1 scoop vanilla protein powder
- 1 cup unsweetened almond milk
- 1 tablespoon almond butter
- 1 teaspoon honey (optional)
- Ice cubes (optional)

Instructions:

1. Fill a blender with all the ingredients.
2. Blend until smooth and well-combined.
3. Ice cubes may be added for a thicker consistency, and the blender runs again.
4. Pour into a glass, then take a sip.

BANANA OATMEAL BREAKFAST SMOOTHIE

Ingredients:

- 1 ripe banana
- 1/2 cup rolled oats
- 1 cup unsweetened almond milk
- 1 tablespoon honey or maple syrup
- 1/2 teaspoon cinnamon
- Ice cubes (optional)

Instructions:

1. Fill a blender with all the ingredients.
2. Blend the mixture until it's creamy and smooth.
3. For a cooled smoothie, if preferred, add ice cubes and blend again.
4. Pour into a glass, then take a sip.

KALE AND APPLE SLIMMING ELIXIR

Ingredients:
- 1 cup kale leaves
- 1 green apple, cored and chopped
- 1/2 cup cucumber, chopped
- 1/2 lemon, juiced
- 1-inch piece of ginger peeled
- 1 cup coconut water
- Ice cubes (optional)

Instructions:
1. Fill a blender with all the ingredients.
2. Blend until thoroughly integrated and smooth.
3. For a cool, refreshing drink, ice cubes may be added and blended again.
4. Pour into a glass, then take a sip.

CUCUMBER MINT SLIMMING REFRESHER

Ingredients:

- 1 cucumber, chopped
- 1/4 cup fresh mint leaves
- 1/2 lemon, juiced
- 2 cups water
- Ice cubes

Instructions:

1. Combine the cucumber, mint leaves, lemon juice, and water in a blender.
2. Puree until combined and well-blended.
3. Fill a glass with ice cubes.
4. Scoop the liquid over the ice.
5. Stir thoroughly, then indulge!

CHOCOLATE PEANUT BUTTER SLIMMING SMOOTHIE

Ingredients:

- 1 cup unsweetened almond milk
- 1 ripe banana
- 2 tablespoons cocoa powder
- 2 tablespoons peanut butter
- 1 tablespoon honey or maple syrup
- Ice cubes (optional)

Instructions:

1. Fill a blender with all the ingredients.
2. Blend until incorporated and creamy.
3. Ice cubes may be added for a thicker consistency, and the blender runs again.
4. Pour into a glass, then take a sip.

SPINACH PINEAPPLE SLIMMING SMOOTHIE

Ingredients:
- 2 cups spinach
- 1 cup frozen pineapple chunks
- 1 ripe banana
- 1/2 cup unsweetened coconut milk
- 1 tablespoon chia seeds
- Ice cubes (optional)

Instructions:
1. Fill a blender with all the ingredients.
2. Blend until creamy and smooth.
3. Enjoy!

BERRY CHIA SLIMMING SHAKE

Ingredients:
- 1 cup mixed berries (strawberries, blueberries, raspberries)
- 1 tablespoon chia seeds
- 1 scoop vanilla protein powder

- 1 cup unsweetened almond milk
- 1 tablespoon honey or maple syrup
- Ice cubes (optional)

Instructions:

1. Fill a blender with all the ingredients.
2. Blend until smooth and well-combined.
3. Ice cubes may be added for a thicker consistency, and the blender runs again.
4. Pour into a glass, then take a sip.

COCONUT BERRY SLIMMING SMOOTHIE

Ingredients:

- 1 cup mixed berries (strawberries, blueberries, raspberries)
- 1/2 cup coconut milk
- 1/2 cup unsweetened almond milk
- 1 tablespoon shredded coconut
- 1 tablespoon chia seeds
- Ice cubes (optional)

Instructions:

1. Fill a blender with all the ingredients.
2. Blend until creamy and smooth.
3. For a cooled smoothie, if preferred, add ice cubes and blend again.
4. Pour into a glass, then take a sip.

MANGO GINGER SLIMMING ELIXIR

Ingredients:

- 1 ripe mango, peeled and pitted
- 1-inch piece of ginger peeled
- 1/2 cup coconut water
- 1/2 cup unsweetened almond milk
- 1 tablespoon honey or maple syrup
- Ice cubes (optional)

Instructions:

1. Fill a blender with all the ingredients.
2. Blend until thoroughly integrated and smooth.
3. For a cool, refreshing drink, ice cubes may be added and blended again.
4. Pour into a glass, then take a sip.

ALMOND BUTTER GREEN SLIMMING SMOOTHIE

Ingredients:

- 2 cups spinach
- 1 ripe banana
- 1 tablespoon almond butter
- 1 cup unsweetened almond milk
- 1 tablespoon honey or maple syrup
- Ice cubes (optional)

Instructions:

1. Fill a blender with all the ingredients.
2. Blend until incorporated and creamy.
3. Ice cubes may be added for a thicker consistency, and the blender runs again.
4. Pour into a glass, then take a sip.

CITRUS GINGER SLIMMING REFRESHER

Ingredients:
- 1 orange, peeled and segmented
- 1/2 lemon, juiced
- 1/2 lime, juiced
- 1-inch piece of ginger peeled
- 2 cups water
- Ice cubes

Instructions:
1. Combine the orange segments, water, ginger, lemon, lime, and oil in a blender.
2. Puree until combined and well-blended.
3. Fill a glass with ice cubes.
4. Scoop the liquid over the ice.
5. Stir thoroughly, then indulge!

BANANA SPLIT SMOOTHIE

Ingredients:

- 1 ripe banana
- 1 cup frozen strawberries
- 1 cup vanilla yogurt
- 1 cup milk
- 1 tablespoon chocolate syrup
- 1 tablespoon chopped walnuts
- Whipped cream and maraschino cherries for garnish

Instructions:

1. Combine the frozen strawberries, vanilla yogurt, ripe banana, milk, and chocolate syrup in a blender.
2. Blend until creamy and smooth.
3. Ladle the smoothie into cups.
4. Finish each glass with whipped cream, chopped walnuts, and a maraschino cherry.
5. Present and savor!

CHOCOLATE BANANA MONKEY SHAKE

Ingredients:

- 2 ripe bananas
- 2 cups milk

- 2 tablespoons chocolate syrup
- 1 cup vanilla ice cream
- Whipped cream and chocolate shavings for garnish

Instructions:

1. Peel the ripe bananas, then chop them up.
2. Combine the vanilla ice cream, milk, chocolate syrup, and banana chunks in a blender.
3. Blend until thoroughly integrated and smooth.
4. Fill the cups with the shake.
5. Place whipped cream over the top and garnish with chocolate shavings.
6. Dish out and savor!

STRAWBERRY SHORTCAKE SMOOTHIE

Ingredients:

- 1 cup frozen strawberries
- 1 cup vanilla yogurt
- 1/2 cup milk
- 1/4 cup crushed graham crackers
- Whipped cream for garnish

Instructions:

1. In a blender, combine milk, vanilla yogurt, and frozen strawberries.
2. Blend until creamy and smooth.
3. Add the crumbled Graham Crackers to the blender, then pulse the machine twice to mix them into the smoothie.
4. Fill the glasses with the smoothie.
5. Add some whipped cream on top.

6. Dish out and savor!

GREEN MONSTER SMOOTHIE

Ingredients:
- 2 cups spinach leaves
- 1 ripe banana
- 1 cup pineapple chunks
- 1 cup almond milk
- 1 tablespoon honey
- Ice cubes (optional)

Instructions:
1. Combine the spinach leaves, ripe banana, chunks of pineapple, almond milk, and honey in a blender.
2. Blend the smoothie until it is smooth, and the ingredients are thoroughly incorporated.
3. Include some ice cubes and mix once more until cold and smooth.
4. Fill glasses with the green monster smoothie.
5. Present and savor!

PEANUT BUTTER AND JELLY SMOOTHIE

Ingredients:
- 1/2 cup frozen mixed berries
- 1 ripe banana
- 2 tablespoons peanut butter
- 1 cup milk

- 1 tablespoon honey (optional)
- Crushed peanuts for garnish

Instructions:

1. Blend the frozen mixed berries, ripe banana, milk, peanut butter, and honey (if using) in a blender.
2. Blend until creamy and smooth.
3. Ladle the smoothie into cups.
4. As a garnish, add some crushed peanuts to the dish.
5. Present and savor!

BLUEBERRY BLASTOFF SMOOTHIE

Ingredients:

- 1 cup frozen blueberries
- 1 ripe banana
- 1/2 cup vanilla yogurt
- 1/2 cup orange juice
- 1 tablespoon honey
- Ice cubes (optional)

Instructions:

1. Combine the frozen blueberries, bananas, orange juice, honey, and vanilla yogurt in a blender.
2. Blend until thoroughly integrated and smooth.
3. Include some ice cubes and mix once more until cold and smooth.
4. Pour glasses with the blueberry Blastoff smoothie.
5. Present and savor!

MANGO PEACH SUNRISE SMOOTHIE

Ingredients:
- 1 ripe mango, peeled and pitted
- 1 ripe peach, peeled and pitted
- 1/2 cup orange juice
- 1/2 cup coconut water
- 1/4 cup Greek yogurt
- Ice cubes (optional)

Instructions:
1. Cut the peach and mango into bits.
2. Combine Greek yogurt, orange juice, peach, mango, and coconut water chunks in a blender.
3. Blend until creamy and smooth.
4. Include some ice cubes and mix once more until cold and smooth.
5. Pour glasses with the mango-peach morning smoothie.
6. Dish out and savor!

APPLE CINNAMON CRUNCH SMOOTHIE

Ingredients:
- 1 medium apple, peeled, cored, and chopped
- 1/2 cup vanilla yogurt
- 1/2 cup almond milk
- 1/4 cup rolled oats
- 1 tablespoon honey
- 1/2 teaspoon cinnamon

- Ice cubes (optional)

Instructions:

1. Combine the diced apple, vanilla yogurt, almond milk, rolled oats, honey, and cinnamon in a blender.
2. Blend until thoroughly integrated and smooth.
3. Include some ice cubes and mix once more until cold and smooth.
4. Pour glasses with the apple cinnamon crunch smoothie inside.
5. Present and savor!

WATERMELON BERRY BLAST

Ingredients:

- 2 cups diced watermelon
- 1 cup frozen mixed berries
- 1/2 cup coconut water
- 1 tablespoon lime juice
- Fresh mint leaves for garnish

Instructions:

1. Blend the coconut water, lime juice, frozen mixed berries, and chopped watermelon together in a blender.
2. Blend thoroughly and smoothly.
3. Fill glasses with the watermelon berry blast.
4. Add fresh mint leaves as a garnish.
5. Present and savor!

ORANGE CREAMSICLE SMOOTHIE

Ingredients:

- 1 cup orange juice
- 1/2 cup vanilla ice cream
- 1/4 cup milk
- 1/2 teaspoon vanilla extract
- Whipped cream and orange zest for garnish

Instructions:

1. Combine the orange juice, milk, vanilla ice cream, and vanilla extract in a blender.
2. Blend until creamy and smooth.
3. Pour glasses with the orange creamsicle smoothie inside.
4. Place whipped cream on top, then garnish with orange zest.
5. Present and savor!

ACAI BERRY BOWL

Ingredients:

- 2 frozen acai packets
- 1/2 cup frozen mixed berries
- 1/2 banana
- 1/2 cup almond milk or your preferred milk
- 1 tablespoon honey or sweetener of your choice
- Toppings: granola, sliced banana, fresh berries, coconut flakes, chia seeds

Instructions:

1. Combine the almond milk, honey, frozen acai packets, frozen mixed berries, and banana in a blender.
2. Blend until creamy and smooth, adding milk to reach the desired consistency.
3. Transfer the substance into a basin.
4. Add granola, banana slices, fresh berries, coconut flakes, and chia seeds as garnishes.
5. Immediately serve and savor!

GREEN GODDESS BOWL

Ingredients:

- 2 cups spinach
- 1/2 avocado
- 1/2 cup cucumber, chopped
- 1/2 cup pineapple chunks
- 1/2 cup coconut water or your preferred liquid
- Juice of 1/2 lime
- Toppings: sliced avocado, hemp seeds, sliced cucumber, microgreens

Instructions:

1. Combine the spinach, coconut water, avocado, cucumber, pineapple pieces, and lime juice in a blender.
2. Blend until creamy and smooth.
3. Transfer the substance into a basin.
4. Add hemp seeds, sliced cucumber, microgreens, and avocado slices.
5. Immediately serve and savor!

MANGO COCONUT BLISS BOWL

Ingredients:

- 1 cup frozen mango chunks
- 1/2 cup coconut milk
- 1/2 banana
- 1 tablespoon shredded coconut
- 1 tablespoon chia seeds

- Toppings: fresh mango slices, coconut flakes, granola, chopped nuts

Instructions:

1. Combine the frozen mango chunks, coconut milk, banana, coconut shreds, and chia seeds in a blender.
2. Blend until creamy and smooth.
3. Transfer the substance into a basin.
4. Add granola, coconut flakes, chopped almonds, and fresh mango slices.
5. Immediately serve and savor!

BERRY BANANA CRUNCH BOWL

Ingredients:

- 1 cup frozen mixed berries
- 1/2 banana
- 1/2 cup Greek yogurt or plant-based yogurt
- 1/4 cup granola
- 1 tablespoon honey or sweetener of your choice
- Toppings: fresh berries, sliced banana, granola, almond slices

Instructions:

1. Combine the frozen mixed berries, Greek yogurt, banana, and honey in a blender until smooth.
2. Transfer the substance into a basin.
3. Add fresh fruit, banana slices, granola, and almond slices over the top.
4. Immediately serve and savor!

CHOCOLATE PEANUT BUTTER BOWL

Ingredients:

- 2 frozen bananas
- 2 tablespoons cocoa powder
- 2 tablespoons peanut butter
- 1/2 cup almond milk or your preferred milk
- 1 tablespoon honey or sweetener of your choice
- Toppings: sliced bananas, crushed peanuts, chocolate chips, a drizzle of peanut butter

Instructions:

1. Combine the honey, almond milk, chocolate powder, peanut butter, and frozen bananas in a blender.
2. Blend until creamy and smooth.
3. Transfer the substance into a basin.
4. Add chopped peanuts, chocolate chips, sliced bananas, and a peanut butter drizzle on top.
5. Immediately serve and savor!

TROPICAL PARADISE BOWL

Ingredients:

- 1 cup frozen pineapple chunks
- 1/2 cup frozen mango chunks
- 1/2 banana
- 1/2 cup coconut water or your preferred liquid
- 1 tablespoon lime juice

- Toppings: sliced kiwi, diced pineapple, shredded coconut, mint leaves

Instructions:

1. Puree the frozen mango, pineapple, and banana with the lime juice and coconut water in a blender.
2. Transfer the substance into a basin.
3. Add mint leaves, chopped pineapple, shredded coconut, and kiwi slices.
4. Immediately serve and savor!

DRAGON FRUIT DELIGHT BOWL

Ingredients:

- 1 cup frozen dragon fruit chunks
- 1/2 cup frozen strawberries
- 1/2 banana
- 1/2 cup almond milk or your preferred milk
- 1 tablespoon honey or sweetener of your choice
- Toppings: sliced dragon fruit, fresh berries, coconut flakes, chia seeds

Instructions:

1. Combine the strawberries, banana, almond milk, honey, and frozen dragon fruit chunks in a blender.
2. Blend until creamy and smooth.
3. Transfer the substance into a basin.
4. Add fresh berries, coconut flakes, chia seeds, and thinly sliced dragon fruit.
5. Immediately serve and savor!

BLUEBERRY ALMOND BOWL

Ingredients:

- 1 cup frozen blueberries
- 1/2 cup almond milk or your preferred milk
- 1/4 cup Greek yogurt or plant-based yogurt
- 1/4 cup almond butter
- 1 tablespoon honey or sweetener of your choice
- Toppings: fresh blueberries, sliced almonds, granola, a drizzle of almond butter

Instructions:

1. Blend the honey, almond butter, Greek yogurt, almond milk, and frozen blueberries until smooth.
2. Transfer the substance into a basin.
3. Add granola, almond butter, sliced fresh blueberries, and sliced almonds over the top.
4. Immediately serve and savor!

KIWI LIME BOWL

Ingredients:

- 2 kiwis, peeled and frozen
- 1/2 banana
- 1/2 cup coconut water or your preferred liquid
- Juice of 1 lime
- 1 tablespoon honey or sweetener of your choice
- Toppings: sliced kiwi, lime zest, shredded coconut, pumpkin seeds

Instructions:

1. Blend the coconut water, lime juice, frozen kiwis, banana, and honey until smooth.
2. Transfer the substance into a basin.
3. Add sliced kiwi, lime zest, coconut shavings, and pumpkin seeds as garnishes.
4. Immediately serve and savor!

PEACH RASPBERRY SWIRL BOWL

Ingredients:

- 1 cup frozen peaches
- 1/2 cup frozen raspberries
- 1/2 banana
- 1/2 cup almond milk or your preferred milk
- 1 tablespoon honey or sweetener of your choice
- Toppings: fresh peach slices, fresh raspberries, granola, a drizzle of honey

Instructions:

1. Combine the almond milk, honey, banana, frozen peaches, and raspberries in a blender.
2. Blend until creamy and smooth.
3. Transfer the substance into a basin.
4. Add granola, raspberries, fresh peach slices, and honey on top.
5. Immediately serve and savor!

SPIRULINA BOWL

Ingredients:

- 2 frozen bananas
- 1 tablespoon spirulina powder
- 1/2 cup almond milk or your preferred milk
- 1 tablespoon honey or sweetener of your choice
- Toppings: sliced kiwi, sliced banana, hemp seeds, coconut flakes

Instructions:

1. Use a blender to thoroughly combine the frozen bananas, spirulina powder, almond milk, and honey.
2. Transfer the substance into a basin.
3. Add hemp seeds, coconut flakes, sliced banana, and kiwi to the top.
4. Immediately serve and savor!

POMEGRANATE SMOOTHIE BOWL

Ingredients:

- 1 cup frozen pomegranate seeds
- 1/2 cup frozen berries (such as strawberries or blueberries)
- 1/2 banana
- 1/2 cup almond milk or your preferred milk
- 1 tablespoon honey or sweetener of your choice
- Toppings: fresh pomegranate seeds, sliced banana, granola, chia seeds

Instructions:

1. Combine the frozen berries, pomegranate seeds, banana, almond milk, and honey in a blender.
2. Blend until creamy and smooth.
3. Transfer the substance into a basin.
4. Add fresh pomegranate, banana slices, granola, and chia seeds as garnish.
5. Immediately serve and savor!

MIXED BERRY BOWL

Ingredients:

- 1 cup mixed frozen berries (such as strawberries, blueberries, and raspberries)
- 1/2 banana
- 1/2 cup Greek yogurt or plant-based yogurt
- 1/4 cup almond milk or your preferred milk
- 1 tablespoon honey or sweetener of your choice
- Toppings: fresh berries, sliced banana, granola, coconut flakes

Instructions:

1. Blend the Greek yogurt, banana, mixed frozen berries, almond milk, and honey until smooth.
2. Transfer the substance into a basin.
3. Sprinkle fresh fruit, banana slices, granola, and coconut flakes over the top. And save.

MATCHA GREEN TEA BOWL

Ingredients:

- 2 teaspoons matcha green tea powder
- 2 frozen bananas
- 1/2 cup almond milk or your preferred milk
- 1 tablespoon honey or sweetener of your choice
- Toppings: sliced strawberries, sliced banana, chia seeds, almond slices

Instructions:

1. Combine the frozen bananas, almond milk, honey, and matcha green tea powder in a blender.
2. Blend until creamy and smooth.
3. Transfer the substance into a basin.
4. Add almond, banana, chia seeds, and strawberry slices on top.
5. Immediately serve and savor!

STRAWBERRIES AND CREAM SMOOTHIE

Ingredients:

- 1 cup strawberries
- 1 cup milk (dairy or plant-based)
- 1/2 cup Greek yogurt
- 1 tablespoon honey or sweetener of choice
- 1/2 teaspoon vanilla extract
- Ice cubes (optional)

Instructions:

1. The strawberries should be cleaned and hulled before being put in a blender.
2. Include the milk, Greek yogurt, honey, vanilla, and (if preferred) ice cubes.
3. Blend until creamy and smooth.
4. Transfer to a glass and serve right away.

MINT CHOCOLATE CHIP SHAKE

Ingredients:

- 2 cups vanilla ice cream
- 1 cup milk (dairy or plant-based)
- 1/2 teaspoon mint extract
- 1/4 cup chocolate chips

- Whipped cream (optional)
- Chocolate syrup (optional)

Instructions:

1. Combine the chocolate chips, mint extract, milk, and vanilla ice cream in a blender.
2. Blend until creamy and smooth.
3. Fill the glass with the shake.
4. If wanted, sprinkle some chocolate syrup over the whipped cream on top.
5. Serve right away.

PUMPKIN PIE SMOOTHIE

Ingredients:

- 1 cup canned pumpkin puree
- 1 cup milk (dairy or plant-based)
- 1 ripe banana
- 2 tablespoons maple syrup
- 1/2 teaspoon pumpkin pie spice
- Ice cubes (optional)
- Whipped cream (optional)
- Ground cinnamon (optional)

Instructions:

1. Combine the milk, banana, maple syrup, pumpkin pie spice, and (if preferred) ice cubes with the pumpkin puree in a blender.
2. Blend until smooth and well-combined.
3. Fill the glass with the smoothie.

4. If preferred, garnish with whipped cream and crushed cinnamon.
5. Offer cold.

BLUEBERRY CHEESECAKE DELIGHT

Ingredients:
- 1 cup fresh or frozen blueberries
- 1 cup milk (dairy or plant-based)
- 1/2 cup cream cheese
- 2 tablespoons honey or sweetener of choice
- 1/2 teaspoon vanilla extract
- Graham cracker crumbs (for garnish)

Instructions:
1. Blend the milk, cream cheese, honey, and vanilla extract with the blueberries.
2. Blend until creamy and smooth.
3. Fill the glass with the smoothie.
4. As a finishing touch, scatter graham cracker crumbs on top.
5. Serve right away.

KEY LIME PIE SMOOTHIE

Ingredients:

- Juice and zest of 2 limes
- 1 cup vanilla yogurt
- 1/2 cup milk (dairy or plant-based)
- 2 tablespoons honey or sweetener of choice
- 1/2 teaspoon vanilla extract
- Ice cubes (optional)
- Whipped cream (optional)
- Lime slices (for garnish)

Instructions:

1. Combine the milk, honey, lime juice, zest, vanilla essence, and ice cubes (if desired) in a blender.
2. Blend until it's creamy and smooth.
3. Fill the glass with the smoothie.
4. If preferred, garnish with lime slices and top with whipped cream.
5. Present cold.

SALTED CARAMEL BANANA SHAKE

Ingredients:

- 2 ripe bananas
- 1 cup milk (dairy or plant-based)
- 2 tablespoons salted caramel sauce
- 1/2 teaspoon vanilla extract
- Ice cubes (optional)

- Whipped cream (optional)
- Caramel drizzle (optional)

Instructions:

1. Slice and peel the bananas.
2. Combine the milk, salted caramel sauce, vanilla extract, and frozen cubes (if using) in a blender. Add the banana slices last.
3. Blend until creamy and smooth.
4. Fill the glass with the shake.
5. If desired, sprinkle some caramel sauce over the whipped cream on top.
6. Serve right away.

COOKIES AND CREAM DREAM

Ingredients:

- 2 cups vanilla ice cream
- 1 cup milk (dairy or plant-based)
- 4 chocolate sandwich cookies
- Whipped cream (optional)
- Crushed cookies (optional)

Instructions:

1. Combine the milk, chocolate sandwich cookies, and vanilla ice cream in a blender.
2. Blend the drink until it is smooth, and the cookies have been entirely integrated.
3. Fill the glass with the shake.
4. If preferred, garnish with whipped cream and crushed cookies.

5. Serve right away.

PEACH COBBLER SMOOTHIE

Ingredients:
- 1 cup frozen peaches
- 1/2 cup vanilla yogurt
- 1/2 cup milk (dairy or plant-based)
- 2 tablespoons honey or sweetener of choice
- 1/2 teaspoon cinnamon
- 1/4 teaspoon nutmeg
- Granola (for garnish)

Instructions:
1. Mash together the frozen peaches, vanilla yogurt, milk, honey, cinnamon, and nutmeg in a blender.
2. Blend until creamy and smooth.
3. Fill the glass with the smoothie.
4. As a garnish, top with granola.
5. Offer cold.

CHOCOLATE RASPBERRY TRUFFLE SMOOTHIE

Ingredients:
- 1 cup frozen raspberries
- 1 cup milk (dairy or plant-based)
- 2 tablespoons cocoa powder
- 2 tablespoons honey or sweetener of choice

- 1/2 teaspoon vanilla extract
- Whipped cream (optional)
- Chocolate shavings (optional)

Instructions:

1. Combine the milk, cocoa powder, honey, and vanilla essence in a blender with the frozen raspberries.
2. Blend until creamy and smooth.
3. Fill the glass with the smoothie.
4. If preferred, garnish with chocolate shavings and whipped cream.
5. Offer cold.

APPLE PIE SMOOTHIE

Ingredients:

- 1 cup chopped apples
- 1/2 cup applesauce
- 1 cup milk (dairy or plant-based)
- 1/4 cup rolled oats
- 2 tablespoons honey or sweetener of choice
- 1/2 teaspoon cinnamon
- Ice cubes (optional)
- Whipped cream (optional)
- Cinnamon stick (for garnish)

Instructions:

1. Combine the applesauce, milk, oats, honey, cinnamon, and ice cubes (if desired) in a blender.
2. Blend until creamy and smooth.
3. Fill the glass with the smoothie.

4. Add whipped cream over the top, and garnish with a cinnamon stick if desired.
5. Offer cold.

COCONUT CREAM PIE SMOOTHIE

Ingredients:
- 1 cup coconut milk
- 1/2 cup Greek yogurt
- 1/2 cup shredded coconut
- 2 tablespoons honey or sweetener of choice
- 1/2 teaspoon vanilla extract
- Ice cubes (optional)
- Whipped cream (optional)
- Toasted coconut flakes (for garnish)

Instructions:
1. Blend the coconut milk, Greek yogurt, coconut shreds, honey, vanilla essence, and ice cubes (if using) in a blender.
2. Blend until creamy and smooth.
3. Fill the glass with the smoothie.
4. Add whipped cream on top, and, if you like, decorate with toasted coconut flakes.
5. Offer cold.

MOCHA ALMOND FUDGE SMOOTHIE

Ingredients:

- 1 cup cold brew coffee
- 1/2 cup almond milk
- 2 tablespoons cocoa powder
- 2 tablespoons almond butter
- 2 tablespoons honey or sweetener of choice
- Ice cubes (optional)
- Whipped cream (optional)
- Chocolate syrup (optional)

Instructions:

1. Combine the almond milk, cold brew coffee, chocolate powder, almond butter, honey, and ice cubes (if preferred) in a blender.
2. Blend until creamy and smooth.
3. Fill the glass with the smoothie.
4. If wanted, sprinkle some chocolate syrup over the whipped cream on top.
5. Offer cold.

BLACK FOREST SMOOTHIE

Ingredients:

- 1 cup frozen cherries
- 1 cup milk (dairy or plant-based)
- 1/4 cup Greek yogurt
- 2 tablespoons cocoa powder
- 2 tablespoons honey or sweetener of choice
- Whipped cream (optional)
- Chocolate shavings (optional)

Instructions:

1. Blend the milk, Greek yogurt, cocoa powder, honey, and frozen cherries.
2. Blend until creamy and smooth.
3. Fill the glass with the smoothie.
4. If preferred, garnish with chocolate shavings and whipped cream.
5. Offer cold.

LEMON MERINGUE SMOOTHIE

Ingredients:

- Juice and zest of 2 lemons
- 1 cup vanilla yogurt
- 1/2 cup milk (dairy or plant-based)
- 2 tablespoons honey or sweetener of choice
- 1/2 teaspoon vanilla extract
- Ice cubes (optional)

- Whipped cream (optional)
- Lemon zest (for garnish)

Instructions:

1. Combine the milk, honey, vanilla extract, lemon juice, lemon zest, and ice cubes (if preferred) in a blender.
2. Blend until creamy and smooth.
3. Fill the glass with the smoothie.
4. Add whipped cream on top, and, if you like, decorate with lemon zest.
5. Offer cold.

PIÑA COLADA SMOOTHIE

Ingredients:

- 1 cup pineapple chunks
- 1/2 cup coconut milk
- 1/2 cup Greek yogurt
- 1 tablespoon honey (optional)
- 1 cup ice cubes

Instructions:

1. Fill a blender with all the ingredients.
2. Blend until creamy and smooth.
3. Pour the mixture into a glass to serve.

MANGO TANGO SMOOTHIE

Ingredients:

- 1 cup mango chunks
- 1/2 cup orange juice
- 1/2 cup plain yogurt
- 1 tablespoon honey (optional)
- 1 cup ice cubes

Instructions:

1. Blend all the ingredients.

2. Purée until foamy and smooth.
3. Pour into a glass, then take a sip.

TROPICAL SUNSHINE SMOOTHIE

Ingredients:

- 1 cup pineapple chunks
- 1/2 cup mango chunks
- 1/2 cup orange juice
- 1/4 cup coconut milk
- 1 tablespoon lime juice
- 1 cup ice cubes

Instructions:

1. Fill a blender with all the ingredients.
2. Blend until creamy and smooth.
3. Pour the mixture into a glass to serve.

PASSIONFRUIT PARADISE SMOOTHIE

Ingredients:

- 1 cup passionfruit pulp
- 1/2 cup pineapple chunks
- 1/2 cup orange juice
- 1/4 cup coconut water
- 1 tablespoon honey (optional)
- 1 cup ice cubes

Instructions:

1. Fill a blender with all the ingredients.
2. Blend until smooth and well-combined.
3. Pour into a glass, then take a sip.

GUAVA COCONUT DELIGHT

Ingredients:

- 1 cup guava chunks
- 1/2 cup coconut milk
- 1/2 cup Greek yogurt
- 1 tablespoon honey (optional)
- 1 cup ice cubes

Instructions:

1. Fill a blender with all the ingredients.
2. Blend until smooth and creamy.
3. Pour the mixture into a glass to serve.

KIWI PAPAYA BURST

Ingredients:

- 1 kiwi, peeled and sliced
- 1/2 cup papaya chunks
- 1/2 cup orange juice
- 1/4 cup Greek yogurt
- 1 tablespoon honey (optional)
- 1 cup ice cubes

Instructions:

1. Blend all the ingredients.
2. Blend until smooth and well-combined.
3. Pour into a glass, then take a sip.

DRAGON FRUIT DREAM SMOOTHIE

Ingredients:
- 1 cup dragon fruit chunks
- 1/2 cup coconut water
- 1/2 cup pineapple juice
- 1 tablespoon lime juice
- 1 tablespoon honey (optional)
- 1 cup ice cubes

Instructions:
1. Fill a blender with all the ingredients.
2. Blend until creamy and smooth.
3. Pour the mixture into a glass to serve.

PINEAPPLE MINT MOJITO SMOOTHIE

Ingredients:
- 1 cup pineapple chunks
- 1/4 cup fresh mint leaves
- 1/2 cup lime juice
- 1/4 cup honey
- 1/2 cup coconut water
- 1 cup ice cubes

Instructions:

1. Fill a blender with all the ingredients.
2. Blend until smooth and well-combined.
3. Pour into a glass, then take a sip.

COCONUT LIME REFRESHER

Ingredients:

- 1 cup coconut water
- 1/2 cup lime juice
- 2 tablespoons honey
- 1/2 teaspoon grated lime zest
- 1 cup ice cubes

Instructions:

1. 2. Use a blender to combine all the items.
2. Blend until smooth and thoroughly incorporated.
3. Pour the liquid into a glass to serve.

LYCHEE BERRY BLISS SMOOTHIE

Ingredients:

- 1 cup lychee fruit, peeled and pitted
- 1/2 cup mixed berries (such as strawberries, raspberries, or blueberries)
- 1/2 cup almond milk
- 1 tablespoon honey (optional)
- 1 cup ice cubes

Instructions:

1. Fill a blender with all the ingredients.
2. Blend until creamy and smooth.
3. Pour into a glass, then take a sip.

TANGERINE MANGO MADNESS

Ingredients:

- 1 cup tangerine segments
- 1/2 cup mango chunks
- 1/2 cup orange juice
- 1/4 cup Greek yogurt
- 1 tablespoon honey (optional)
- 1 cup ice cubes

Instructions:

1. Blend all the ingredients.
2. Blend until smooth and well-combined.
3. Pour the mixture into a glass to serve.

KIWI WATERMELON CRUSH

Ingredients:

- 1 kiwi, peeled and sliced
- 1 cup watermelon chunks
- 1/2 cup coconut water
- 1 tablespoon lime juice
- 1 tablespoon honey (optional)
- 1 cup ice cubes

Instructions:

1. Fill a blender with all the ingredients.
2. Purée until foamy and smooth.
3. Pour into a glass, then take a sip.

BANANA GUAVA SMOOTHIE

Ingredients:

- 1 banana
- 1/2 cup guava chunks
- 1/2 cup pineapple juice
- 1/4 cup Greek yogurt
- 1 tablespoon honey (optional)
- 1 cup ice cubes

Instructions:

1. Fill a blender with all the ingredients.
2. Blend until smooth and creamy.
3. Pour the mixture into a glass to serve.

PINEAPPLE GINGER ZING

Ingredients:

- 1 cup pineapple chunks
- 1/2 inch fresh ginger, grated
- 1/2 cup coconut water
- 1 tablespoon lime juice
- 1 tablespoon honey (optional)
- 1 cup ice cubes

Instructions:

1. Blend all the ingredients.
2. Blend until smooth and well-combined.
3. Pour into a glass, then take a sip.

COCONUT KIWI LIME SMOOTHIE

Ingredients:

- 1 kiwi, peeled and sliced
- 1/2 cup coconut milk
- 1/2 cup lime juice
- 1 tablespoon honey (optional)
- 1 cup ice cubes

Instructions:

1. Fill a blender with all the ingredients.
2. Blend until creamy and smooth.
3. Pour the mixture into a glass to serve.

MANGO PINEAPPLE BASIL SMOOTHIE

Ingredients:

- 1 cup mango chunks
- 1/2 cup pineapple chunks
- 1/4 cup fresh basil leaves
- 1/2 cup coconut water
- 1 tablespoon lime juice
- 1 tablespoon honey (optional)
- 1 cup ice cubes

Instructions:

1. Fill a blender with all the ingredients.
2. Blend until smooth and well-combined.
3. Pour into a glass, then take a sip.

CHAPTER 17: SEASONAL SMOOTHIE SPECIALTIES

SPICED PUMPKIN SMOOTHIE

Ingredients:

- 1 cup pumpkin puree
- 1 cup almond milk
- 1 ripe banana
- 1/2 teaspoon cinnamon
- 1/4 teaspoon nutmeg
- 1/4 teaspoon ginger
- 1 tablespoon honey or maple syrup (optional)
- Ice cubes

Instructions:

1. If desired, combine the pumpkin puree, almond milk, banana, cinnamon, nutmeg, ginger, and sweetener in a blender.
2. Blend until creamy and smooth.
3. Add ice cubes and blend until the smoothie has your preferred consistency.
4. Pour the liquid into a glass to serve.

APPLE CINNAMON DELIGHT

Ingredients:

- 1 apple, cored and chopped
- 1 cup almond milk
- 1/2 cup Greek yogurt
- 1/2 teaspoon cinnamon
- 1 tablespoon honey or maple syrup (optional)
- Ice cubes

Instructions:

1. If blending is preferred, combine the Greek yogurt, cinnamon, almond milk, and apple chunks.
2. Blend the ingredients until they are smooth and well combined.
3. Include ice cubes and reblend the smoothie until it is cold and creamy.
4. Pour into a glass, then take a sip.

CRANBERRY ORANGE BURST

Ingredients:

- 1 cup cranberries
- 1 orange, peeled and segmented
- 1 banana
- 1 cup orange juice
- 1/2 cup Greek yogurt
- 1 tablespoon honey or maple syrup (optional)
- Ice cubes

Instructions:

1. Place the banana, orange segments, cranberries, Greek yogurt, orange juice, and any additional sugar in a blender.
2. Continue blending until each component is well combined and creamy.
3. Add the ice cubes and blend the smoothie until it is chilled and creamy.
4. Pour the liquid into a glass to serve.

PEPPERMINT MOCHA SMOOTHIE

Ingredients:

- 1 cup cold brew coffee
- 1/2 cup almond milk
- 1 ripe banana
- 2 tablespoons cocoa powder
- 1/2 teaspoon peppermint extract
- 1 tablespoon honey or maple syrup (optional)
- Ice cubes

Instructions:

1. In a blender, if desired, combine the cold brew coffee, almond milk, banana that has reached peak ripeness, chocolate powder, peppermint essence, and sweetener.
2. Blend the ingredients until they are smooth and well combined.
3. Include ice cubes and re-blend the smoothie until it is cold and foamy.
4. Pour into a glass; if preferred, top with whipped cream and a dash of chocolate powder.

GINGERBREAD COOKIE SHAKE

Ingredients:

- 1 cup almond milk
- 1 ripe banana
- 1 tablespoon molasses
- 1/2 teaspoon ground ginger
- 1/2 teaspoon ground cinnamon
- 1/4 teaspoon ground nutmeg
- 1/4 teaspoon vanilla extract
- 1 tablespoon honey or maple syrup (optional)
- Ice cubes

Instructions:

1. Combine the almond milk, ripe banana, molasses, ground ginger, cinnamon, nutmeg, and sweetener in a blender.
2. Continue blending until all of the ingredients are well combined and smooth.
3. Blend the smoothie again after adding the ice cubes to make it cold and creamy.
4. Pour into a glass; if preferred, top with some ground cinnamon.

BERRY CITRUS SUNSHINE SMOOTHIE

Ingredients:

- 1 cup mixed berries (such as strawberries, blueberries, or raspberries)
- 1 orange, peeled and segmented

- 1/2 cup Greek yogurt
- 1 tablespoon honey or maple syrup (optional)
- Ice cubes

Instructions:

1. If desired, combine the Greek yogurt, mixed berries, orange segments, and sweetener in a blender.
2. Blend the ingredients until they are smooth and well combined.
3. Include ice cubes and reblend the smoothie until it is cold and creamy.
4. Pour into a glass, then take a sip.

SUMMER WATERMELON REFRESHER

Ingredients:

- 2 cups seedless watermelon, cubed
- 1 cup cucumber, peeled and chopped
- Juice of 1 lime
- 1 tablespoon honey or maple syrup (optional)
- Ice cubes
- Fresh mint leaves for garnish (optional)

Instructions:

1. Fill a blender with the watermelon, cucumber, lime juice, and any more sweetness you want.
2. Continue blending until each component is well combined and creamy.
3. Add the ice cubes and blend the smoothie until it is icy and cooling.

4. Pour into a glass, add fresh mint leaves as a garnish, and serve.

MAPLE PECAN SMOOTHIE

Ingredients:
- 1 cup almond milk
- 1 ripe banana
- 2 tablespoons maple syrup
- 2 tablespoons pecans
- 1/4 teaspoon vanilla extract
- 1/4 teaspoon cinnamon
- Ice cubes

Instructions:
1. Combine the almond milk, banana in its ripe state, maple syrup, nuts, vanilla essence, and cinnamon in a blender.
2. Blend the ingredients until they are smooth and well combined.
3. Include ice cubes and reblend the smoothie until it is cold and creamy.
4. Pour into a glass, top with a dash of cinnamon, and sip.

BUTTERNUT SQUASH SPICE SMOOTHIE

Ingredients:
- 1 cup cooked butternut squash, cooled
- 1 cup almond milk
- 1 ripe banana

- 1/2 teaspoon cinnamon
- 1/4 teaspoon nutmeg
- 1 tablespoon honey or maple syrup (optional)
- Ice cubes

Instructions:

1. Butternut squash that has been cooked, almond milk, ripe bananas, cinnamon, nutmeg, and sugar can all be combined in a blender if preferred.
2. Continue blending until each component is well combined and creamy.
3. Include ice cubes and reblend the smoothie until it is cold and creamy.
4. Pour the mixture into a glass, top with a dash of cinnamon, and serve.

FIG AND HONEY BLISS

Ingredients:

- 1 cup almond milk
- 4 fresh figs, stemmed and halved
- 1 ripe banana
- 1 tablespoon honey
- 1/4 teaspoon vanilla extract
- Ice cubes

Instructions:

1. 11. Fill a blender with almond milk, ripe banana, fresh figs, honey, and vanilla essence.
2. 12. Blend everything until it's completely smooth and well-combined.

3. 13. Blend the smoothie again after adding the ice cubes until it is cold and creamy.
4. Pour the mixture into a glass and sip.

CITRUS BEET DETOX SMOOTHIE

Ingredients:
- 1 medium beet, peeled and chopped
- 1 orange, peeled and segmented
- 1/2 grapefruit, peeled and segmented
- 1 cup coconut water
- 1 tablespoon honey or maple syrup (optional)
- Ice cubes

Instructions:
1. If desired, combine the coconut water, chopped orange, grapefruit, and sweetener in a blender.
2. Blend the ingredients until they are smooth and well combined.
3. Include ice cubes and reblend the smoothie until it is cold and creamy.
4. Pour the liquid into a glass to serve.

CARAMEL APPLE DELIGHT

Ingredients:
- 1 apple, cored and chopped
- 1 cup almond milk
- 2 tablespoons caramel sauce

- 1/4 teaspoon cinnamon
- 1 tablespoon honey or maple syrup (optional)
- Ice cubes

Instructions:

1. If desired, combine the apple chunks, almond milk, caramel sauce, cinnamon, and sweetener in a blender.
2. Continue blending until each component is well combined and creamy.
3. Include ice cubes and reblend the smoothie until it is cold and creamy.
4. If you'd like, pour it into a glass, top with more caramel sauce, and sip.

WINTER SPICE SMOOTHIE

Ingredients:

- 1 cup almond milk
- 1/2 cup plain Greek yogurt
- 1 ripe banana
- 1/2 teaspoon cinnamon
- 1/4 teaspoon nutmeg
- 1/4 teaspoon cloves
- 1 tablespoon honey or maple syrup (optional)
- Ice cubes

Instructions:

1. Fill a blender with the Greek yogurt, cinnamon, nutmeg, cloves, almond milk, ripe banana, and additional sugar, if desired.

2. Blend the ingredients until they are smooth and well combined.
3. Add the ice cubes and process the smoothie until it is cold and creamy.
4. Pour the mixture into a glass, top with a dash of cinnamon, and serve.

EGGNOG SMOOTHIE

Ingredients:

- 1 cup almond milk
- 1 ripe banana
- 1/4 teaspoon nutmeg
- 1/4 teaspoon cinnamon
- 1 tablespoon honey or maple syrup (optional)
- Ice cubes

Instructions:

1. If desired, combine the almond milk, ripe banana, nutmeg, cinnamon, and sweetener in a blender.
2. Continue blending until each component is well combined and creamy.
3. Include ice cubes and reblend the smoothie until it is cold and creamy.
4. Pour into a glass, top with a dash of nutmeg, and savor.

CRANBERRY PEAR REFRESHER

Ingredients:

- 1 cup cranberries
- 1 ripe pear, cored and chopped
- 1 cup apple juice
- 1/2 cup Greek yogurt
- 1 tablespoon honey or maple syrup (optional)
- Ice cubes

Instructions:

1. If desired, combine the Greek yogurt, cranberries, pear chunks, apple juice, and sweetener in a blender.
2. Blend the ingredients until they are smooth and well combined.
3. Include ice cubes and reblend the smoothie until it is cold and creamy.
4. Pour the liquid into a glass to serve.

BANANA BERRY BURST

Ingredients:

- 1 ripe banana
- 1 cup mixed berries (strawberries, blueberries, raspberries)
- 1/2 cup plain Greek yogurt
- 1/2 cup almond milk
- 1 tablespoon honey (optional)

Instructions:

1. Cut the banana into chunks after peeling it.
2. Fill a blender with Greek yogurt, mixed berries, almond milk, and honey (if using).
3. Blend on high power until creamy and smooth.
4. Pour into a glass, then take a sip.

SPINACH MANGO TANGO

Ingredients:

- 1 cup spinach
- 1 ripe mango, peeled and pitted
- 1/2 cup pineapple chunks
- 1/2 cup orange juice
- 1/2 cup coconut water

Instructions:

1. Combine the spinach, mango, chunks of pineapple, orange juice, and coconut water in a blender.
2. Blend at maximum speed until smooth and thoroughly incorporated.
3. Pour into a cold glass and serve.

PEANUT BUTTER BANANA SHAKE

Ingredients:

- 1 ripe banana
- 2 tablespoons peanut butter
- 1 cup milk (dairy or plant-based)
- 1 tablespoon honey (optional)
- Ice cubes (optional)

Instructions:

1. Cut the banana into chunks after peeling it.
2. Fill a blender with the fragments of banana, peanut butter, milk, honey (if preferred), and ice cubes (if used).
3. Combine at a high speed until foamy and creamy.
4. Pour into a glass, then take a sip.

TROPICAL GREEN GODDESS

Ingredients:

- 1 cup spinach
- 1/2 cup chopped pineapple
- 1/2 cup chopped mango

- 1/2 ripe avocado
- 1/2 cup coconut water
- Juice of 1 lime
- Ice cubes (optional)

Instructions:

1. Combine the spinach, lime juice, pineapple, mango, avocado, coconut water, and ice cubes (if preferred) in a blender.
2. Blend until creamy and smooth.
3. Pour into a cold glass and serve.

BLUEBERRY ALMOND BLISS

Ingredients:

- 1 cup blueberries
- 1/4 cup almond butter
- 1 cup almond milk
- 1 tablespoon honey (optional)
- Ice cubes (optional)

Instructions:

1. If using, fill a blender with the blueberries, almond butter, almond milk, honey, and ice cubes.
2. Puree until creamy and well combined.
3. Pour into a glass, then sip.

STRAWBERRY SPINACH SURPRISE

Ingredients:

- 1 cup fresh strawberries
- 1 cup spinach
- 1/2 cup plain Greek yogurt
- 1/2 cup almond milk
- 1 tablespoon chia seeds (optional)

Instructions:

1. Fill a blender with the spinach, strawberries, Greek yogurt, almond milk, and chia seeds (if using).
2. Blend until creamy and smooth.
3. Pour into a cold glass and serve.

GREEN APPLE GINGER ZINGER

Ingredients:

- 1 green apple, cored and chopped
- 1/2 cup spinach
- 1/2-inch piece of fresh ginger, peeled and grated
- Juice of 1 lemon
- 1 cup coconut water
- Ice cubes (optional)

Instructions:

1. In a blender, combine the spinach, green apple, ginger, lemon juice, coconut water, and ice cubes (if using). Blend until smooth.
2. Blend until smooth and thoroughly incorporated.

3. Pour into a glass, then sip.

CHOCOLATE AVOCADO DREAM

Ingredients:

- 1 ripe avocado
- 2 tablespoons unsweetened cocoa powder
- 1 cup milk (dairy or plant-based)
- 2 tablespoons honey or maple syrup
- Ice cubes (optional)

Instructions:

1. Remove the avocado's flesh and put it in a blender.
2. Fill the blender with the cocoa powder, milk, honey or maple syrup, and ice cubes (if using).
3. Blend until creamy and smooth.
4. Pour into a glass, then take a sip.

MANGO COCONUT COOLER

Ingredients:

- 1 ripe mango, peeled and pitted
- 1/2 cup coconut milk
- 1/2 cup pineapple juice
- 1/2 cup plain Greek yogurt
- 1 tablespoon lime juice
- Ice cubes (optional)

Instructions:

1. Chop up the mango and add it to the blender.
2. Fill the blender with coconut milk, pineapple juice, Greek yogurt, lime juice, and (optional) ice cubes.
3. Puree until smooth and thoroughly combined.
4. Pour into a cold glass and serve.

RASPBERRY LIME REFRESHER

Ingredients:

- 1 cup raspberries
- Juice of 2 limes
- 1/2 cup coconut water
- 1 tablespoon honey or agave syrup
- Ice cubes (optional)

Instructions:

1. Combine the raspberries, lime juice, coconut water, honey or agave syrup, and any ice cubes you're using in a blender.
2. Blend until thoroughly integrated and smooth.
3. Pour into a glass, then sip.

PINEAPPLE KALE ENERGIZER

Ingredients:

- 1 cup chopped pineapple
- 1 cup kale leaves
- 1/2 cup orange juice
- 1/2 cup coconut water

- 1 tablespoon fresh mint leaves (optional)
- Ice cubes (optional)

Instructions:

1. Fill a blender with the pineapple, kale leaves, coconut water, orange juice, and fresh mint leaves (if using).
2. Blend until creamy and smooth.
3. Pour into a cold glass and serve.

CUCUMBER MELON FRESHNESS

Ingredients:

- 1 cup chopped cucumber
- 1 cup chopped honeydew melon
- Juice of 1 lime
- 1/2 cup coconut water
- 1 tablespoon fresh mint leaves
- Ice cubes (optional)

Instructions:

1. Combine the cucumber, honeydew melon, coconut water, lime juice, and fresh mint leaves in a blender. Add ice cubes (if preferred).
2. Puree until smooth and thoroughly combined.
3. Pour into a glass, then sip.

MIXED BERRY POWERHOUSE

Ingredients:

- 1 cup mixed berries (strawberries, blueberries, raspberries)
- 1/2 cup plain Greek yogurt
- 1/2 cup almond milk
- 1 tablespoon honey or agave syrup
- 1 tablespoon flaxseeds (optional)
- Ice cubes (optional)

Instructions:

1. In a blender, combine the Greek yogurt, almond milk, honey or agave nectar, flaxseeds (if using), and ice cubes (if wanted). Blend until smooth.
2. Blend until creamy and smooth.
3. Pour into a cold glass and serve.

ORANGE CARROT SUNRISE

Ingredients:

- 1 orange, peeled and segmented
- 1 carrot, peeled and chopped
- 1/2 cup pineapple chunks
- 1/2 cup orange juice
- 1/2 cup coconut water
- Ice cubes (optional)

Instructions:

1. Fill a blender with the orange segments, carrot, pineapple chunks, coconut water, orange juice, and ice cubes (if preferred).
2. Blend until thoroughly integrated and smooth.
3. Pour into a cold glass and serve.

BUILD-YOUR-OWN BERRY BLAST

Ingredients:

- 1 cup mixed berries (such as strawberries, blueberries, and raspberries)
- 1 ripe banana
- 1 cup almond milk (or any other non-dairy milk of your choice)
- 1 tablespoon honey or maple syrup (optional for added sweetness)
- Ice cubes (optional)

Instructions:

1. Clean the berries, taking care to get rid of any stems or leaves.
2. Slice and peel the banana.
3. Put the mixed berries, banana, almond milk, and sweetener (if using) in a blender.
4. Blend on high power until creamy and smooth.
5. If preferred, add ice cubes and blend once more to incorporate fully.
6. Pour the liquid into a glass and serve right away.

PERSONALIZED GREEN POWER SMOOTHIE

Ingredients:

- 2 cups fresh spinach
- 1 ripe banana
- 1/2 ripe avocado
- 1 cup coconut water
- 1 tablespoon chia seeds
- Juice of 1/2 lemon
- Ice cubes (optional)

Instructions:

1. Thoroughly wash the spinach leaves.
2. Slice and peel the banana.
3. Halve the avocado, scoop out the flesh, and discard the pit.
4. Combine the spinach, avocado, banana, coconut water, chia seeds, and lemon juice in a blender.
5. Blend on high power until creamy and smooth.
6. If preferred, add ice cubes and blend one more for optimal mixing.
7. Transfer to a glass and serve right away.

CUSTOMIZABLE PROTEIN-PACKED SHAKE

Ingredients:

- 1 cup unsweetened almond milk (or any other non-dairy milk of your choice)
- 1 scoop protein powder (vanilla, chocolate, or your preferred flavor)
- 1 ripe banana
- 1 tablespoon nut butter (such as almond butter or peanut butter)
- 1 tablespoon honey or maple syrup (optional for added sweetness)
- Ice cubes (optional)

Instructions:

1. Blend the protein powder, ripe banana, nut butter, almond milk, and sweetener (if using) in a blender.
2. Blend at high speed until creamy and well incorporated.
3. Should you choose, add ice cubes and blend once more until smooth.
4. Transfer to a glass and serve right away.

TAILORED DAIRY-FREE DELIGHT

Ingredients:

- 1 cup coconut milk (or any other non-dairy milk of your choice)
- 1/2 cup frozen mango chunks
- 1/2 cup frozen pineapple chunks
- 1 ripe banana

- 1 tablespoon shredded coconut
- 1 tablespoon chia seeds
- Ice cubes (optional)

Instructions:

1. Combine the chia seeds, ripe banana, shredded coconut, frozen mango and pineapple chunks, and coconut milk in a blender.
2. Blend on high power until creamy and smooth.
3. If preferred, add ice cubes and blend one more for optimal mixing.
4. Transfer to a glass and serve right away.

NUT BUTTER AND CHOCOLATE CUSTOM BLEND

Ingredients:

- 1 cup almond milk (or any other non-dairy milk of your choice)
- 2 tablespoons nut butter (such as almond butter or cashew butter)
- 1 tablespoon cocoa powder
- 1 ripe banana
- 1 tablespoon honey or maple syrup (optional for added sweetness)
- Ice cubes (optional)

Instructions:

1. Combine the ripe banana, chocolate powder, nut butter, almond milk, and sweetener (if using).

2. Blend at a high speed until the mixture is smooth and creamy.
3. If preferred, mix again after adding the ice cubes.
4. Fill a glass and serve right away.

SUPERFOOD BOOST YOUR WAY

Ingredients:
- 1 cup almond milk (or any other non-dairy milk of your choice)
- 1 cup fresh or frozen mixed berries
- 1 ripe banana
- 1 tablespoon chia seeds
- 1 tablespoon flaxseeds
- 1 tablespoon hemp seeds
- 1 tablespoon spirulina powder
- Ice cubes (optional)

Instructions:
1. Combine the chia seeds, flaxseeds, hemp seeds, mixed berries, almond milk, and spirulina powder in a blender.
2. Blend at high speed until thoroughly combined and smooth.
3. Include ice cubes and blend one more until you get the desired consistency.
4. Transfer to a glass and serve right away.

DETOX AND CLEANSING ELIXIR TO SUIT YOUR NEEDS

Ingredients:

- 1 cup coconut water
- 1 cucumber, peeled and chopped
- 1 lemon, juiced
- 1-inch fresh ginger peeled
- 1 tablespoon fresh mint leaves
- 1 tablespoon honey or maple syrup (optional for added sweetness)
- Ice cubes (optional)

Instructions:

1. Blend the coconut water, cucumber, ginger, lemon juice, mint leaves, and sweetener (if using) in a blender.
2. Until all the ingredients are thoroughly combined, mix on high speed.
3. If desired, mix again until cold and smooth after adding ice cubes.
4. Transfer to a glass and serve right away.

IMMUNITY-BOOSTING FORMULA, YOUR STYLE

Ingredients:

- 1 cup orange juice
- 1/2 cup plain Greek yogurt (or dairy-free yogurt)
- 1 cup mixed berries (such as strawberries, blueberries, and raspberries)
- 1 ripe banana
- 1 tablespoon honey or maple syrup (optional for added sweetness)
- Ice cubes (optional)

Instructions:

1. Blend the ripe banana, orange juice, Greek yogurt, mixed berries, and sweetener (if using) in a blender.
2. Blend on high power until creamy and smooth.
3. If preferred, add ice cubes and blend one more for optimal mixing.
4. Transfer to a glass and serve right away.

ENERGIZING SMOOTHIE FOR YOUR ACTIVE LIFESTYLE

Ingredients:

- 1 cup unsweetened almond milk (or any other non-dairy milk of your choice)
- 1 ripe banana
- 1/2 cup fresh or frozen berries (such as blueberries or raspberries)
- 1 tablespoon almond butter
- 1 tablespoon honey or maple syrup (optional for added sweetness)
- 1 tablespoon rolled oats
- Ice cubes (optional)

Instructions:

1. In a blender, combine the rolled oats, almond milk, ripe banana, berries, almond butter, and sweetener (if using).
2. Blend at high speed until thoroughly combined and smooth.
3. Include ice cubes and blend one more until you get the desired consistency.
4. Transfer to a glass and serve right away.

WEIGHT MANAGEMENT SMOOTHIE, PERSONALIZED

Ingredients:

- 1 cup unsweetened almond milk (or any other non-dairy milk of your choice)
- 1/2 cup Greek yogurt (or dairy-free yogurt)
- 1 cup spinach leaves
- 1 ripe banana
- 1 tablespoon nut butter (such as almond butter or peanut butter)
- 1 tablespoon flaxseeds
- Ice cubes (optional)

Instructions:

1. Combine the flaxseeds, nut butter, spinach leaves, Greek yogurt, almond milk, and ripe banana in a blender.
2. Until all the ingredients are thoroughly combined, mix on high speed.
3. Add ice cubes and mix one more if preferred to create a chilled, creamy smoothie.
4. Transfer to a glass and serve right away.

KID-FRIENDLY SMOOTHIE ADVENTURE, YOUR CHOICE

Ingredients:

- 1 cup milk (dairy or non-dairy)
- 1 ripe banana
- 1/2 cup frozen fruit (such as strawberries, mango, or pineapple)
- 1 tablespoon honey or maple syrup (optional for added sweetness)
- 1/4 cup yogurt (plain or flavored)
- Ice cubes (optional)

Instructions:

1. In a blender, combine the yogurt, milk, ripe banana, frozen fruit, honey, or maple syrup (if using).
2. Blend on high power until creamy and smooth.
3. If preferred, add ice cubes and blend one more for optimal mixing.
4. Transfer to a glass and serve right away.

PERSONALIZED SMOOTHIE BOWL CREATION

Ingredients:

- 1 ripe banana
- 1/2 cup frozen fruit (such as berries, mango, or pineapple)
- 1/2 cup milk (dairy or non-dairy)
- 1 tablespoon nut butter (such as almond butter or cashew butter)
- Toppings of your choice (such as granola, sliced fruits, coconut flakes, chia seeds, or nuts)

Instructions:

1. Combine the frozen fruit, milk, and nut butter in a blender with the ripe banana.
2. Blend on high power until creamy and smooth.
3. Fill a bowl with the smoothie mixture.
4. Add your preferred toppings to the smoothie bowl for decoration.
5. Immediately serve and eat with a spoon.

CHAPTER 20: NUTRIBULLET SMOOTHIE TIPS AND TRICKS

This book offers helpful hints and shortcuts to improve your smoothie-making efficiency. These suggestions will assist you in making tasty and nutrient-dense smoothies with your Nutribullet blender, from boosting flavor profiles to maximizing nutrient extraction.

Choosing the Correct Cup Size: The appropriate size is crucial for the best blending results. The cup sizes available with the Nutribullet usually range from 18 to 32 ounces. Larger cups are good for several servings or when making smoothies in advance, but smaller cups are perfect for single servings or portion management. The cup size should be adjusted based on your requirements.

Ingredient Layering for Even Blending: It's crucial to layer your components properly for a uniform blend and silky texture. Start by blending the liquid base, such as juice, water, or milk. Then incorporate your leafy greens, produce, fruits, and other ingredients. Through the effective engagement of the blades with the contents, this layering approach makes a well-blended smoothie.

Ingredients for pre-freezing: A game-changer for a cold and refreshing smoothie without ice is to pre-freeze some components. Your smoothie gains thickness and a crisp texture from adding frozen fruit chunks like bananas, berries, and mango. Leafy greens can also be frozen in sections for increased convenience. Ingredients frozen in advance taste better and need less ice, preventing dilution.

Adding the Correct Amount of Liquid: The right amount of liquid you add to your smoothie is essential for getting the right consistency. A tiny amount of liquid, such as water or your favorite liquid base, should be added at first. You can, if necessary, progressively increase the amount based on the required thickness. Adjusting the liquid ensures that your smoothie is the right consistency for the components to combine without being too thick or thin.

Trying Different Flavor Combinations: One of the pleasures of Nutribullet smoothies is the chance to try different flavor combinations. Combine and match various fruits, vegetables, herbs, spices, and other additions to create distinctive and mouthwatering taste profiles. There are countless possible combinations, from traditional ones like strawberry and banana to more daring ones like pineapple and cilantro. Keep a list of your preferred combinations for later use.

Harmonizing Sweet and Tangy: A tasty smoothie must have just the perfect amount of sweetness and tanginess to succeed. Fruits like bananas, cherries, and mangoes can naturally include sweetness, while citrus fruits or a squeeze of lemon or lime juice can add tang. Depending on your preferences, change the proportions of the sweet and sour ingredients to create a balanced flavor profile.

Superfoods' Increased Nutritional Value: Adding Superfoods to Your Smoothies Will Increase Their Nutritional Value: Superfoods are nutrient-dense items that provide your smoothies an added nutritious boost. Take into account adding superfoods to your recipes, such as chia seeds, flaxseeds, hemp hearts, spirulina, acai berries, or matcha powder. These superfoods give your smoothies an additional health boost because they are high in antioxidants, omega-3 fatty acids, vitamins, and minerals.

Enhancing Creaminess and Texture: Consider including items that add richness to your smoothies to obtain a creamy and velvety texture. Excellent alternatives include avocado, Greek yogurt, coconut milk, nut butter, and silken tofu. These ingredients give your smoothie extra creaminess and healthy fats and proteins, which increases satisfaction and nutrition.

THE END

Printed in Great Britain
by Amazon